MW01006195

How to sell
Network
Marketing

without fear, anxiety
or losing your friends!

Selling from the Soul.

Ancient Wisdoms.

Modern Practice.

By Michael Oliver

For information write:
Natural Selling® Inc.
502 N. Division Street
Carson City, Nevada 89703
U.S.A.

1.800.758.6989
1.775.886.0777
E-mail: info@naturalselling.com
Website: http://www.NaturalSelling.com

ISBN: 0-9715889-0-2

Cover design and layout by: Geoff Gosson
Published by: Natural Selling® Inc.
Printed in Canada by Friesens

Find your own truth, by shedding the truths of others that prevent you from having the freedom and abundance that is your universal right.

Natural Selling®

HOW TO SELL NETWORK MARKETING

Table of Contents

Foreword:
Critical Distinctions – Two Truths

One way to change the impossible
is to change the climate.

After 22 years of being in the world of professional selling, I have discovered there is a critical distinction between traditional selling and what I call Natural Selling®.

Traditional selling depends on techniques and systems that persuades people to do what you want them to do (even if you're coming from a place of wanting to help) while Natural Selling® comes from an inner desire to serve and allow others to persuade themselves, *before* presenting your business opportunity.

It's a distinction that, once understood and acted on, will allow you to eliminate the personal discomfort and lack of desire to talk with people about your business or your products that usually comes from the fear of being rejected!

As a result, what you will learn in this book might *change* your outlook on talking with people. It might *strengthen* the way you talk with people if you already follow these principles and methods, and more importantly, it might change your life!

This book will explore with you:

- Why selling in the traditional style can cause tension, for you and the person you're talking with, and almost guarantee to bring resistance in the form of objections.

- Why traditional selling more often than not will cause you to be rejected.

- How you can replace how you're communicating, or how you think you have to communicate, with a different set of behaviors that will make a difference in your ability to help others and substantially increase the results you're looking for.

If you decide to embrace and vigorously *act* on the principles, and people skills, in this book, *you will* receive:

- More positive feedback from people – by having people be attracted and relate to you as opposed to reject you.

- More positive results, as a consequence of changing from a 'me' approach to a 'you and I' approach.

- A greater sense of personal fulfillment and inner calm and peace!

Overview
Natural Selling®

"WHAT DO I DO? WHAT DO I SAY?"

When you start as a distributor in Network Marketing, it's likely you'll ask yourself two questions: *"What do I do?"* and *"What do I say?"*

The first question, *"What do I do?"* is a left-brain, logical, systematic question that has been superbly answered by companies and their distributors with logical solutions. You follow logical duplicable systems that are set in place for you to set goals, create lead generation programs, internally communicate, set procedures to follow, and so on.

The second question, *"What do I say?"* or, to be more precise, *"What do I ask?"* is more of a right-brain activity, which deals with the issue of people skills of *feelings and emotions.*

You've probably heard the expression that people buy on emotion (right-brain) and justify with logic (left-brain). While the two are inseparable, they each require a different understanding and skill.

DOES A ONE-SIZE APPROACH FIT ALL?

Most Network Marketing companies and many distributors answer the training needs of this right-brain activity of communicating (with all of its emotional variances), with a left-brain logical approach.

How often have you heard these phrases: "No selling is involved" – "Just give these tapes away and tell people that what they hear on them will change their lives!" – "It's a numbers game of speaking with as many people as possible and telling your story" – "You just share your story when you meet people!"

While this is an admirable attempt to keep things easy and simple it appears to have a fatal flaw! It's not an acceptable or a comfortable approach for the majority of distributors. The logical approach of telling people things and systemizing a highly personal and interactive activity can be impersonal and adversarial for the person on the receiving end. The fallout from this is a high level of rejection, resulting in increased tension for most distributors and potential customers, followed by a lack of distributor activity and a high attrition rate.

CAN YOU DUPLICATE FEELINGS?

The question is, just because something can be systemized, duplicated and works for a small number of people, does it mean it will work for everyone? (In the next chapter, I talk about the 20/80 Rule that discusses this.)

Also, do logic and/or systems create relationships, which are the foundation of any successful sale and downline organization? Not really! People communicating with people create relationships. To do it effectively requires people skills – skills you either have or must learn.

Interestingly, while some successful distributors teach this systematic logical approach, they don't always use it themselves! So why do they teach it? Because it's easy to teach and easy to learn! Its weakness, however, is that most distributors won't do it. Not that they can't – they won't. Of further interest, even though it appeals only to a minority of people, it has enough success to perpetuate the continuation of it.

SELLING IS NOT A LOGICAL ART!

The art of communicating effectively is not a logical activity. Most people base their decisions on whether to make a change from what they are presently doing, or what products they will buy, not from logic but from feelings and from emotions. Logic very rarely helps people feel the need for things.

Having said that, using a combination of logic and feeling can be quite powerful. For example, the answer to a left-brain question, *"What did you do next when your boss said that to you?"* would probably be a logical step-by-step description of what happened next.

Asking a right-brain question such as, *"And how did you feel about that?"* or, *"How did that affect you and your department?"* will get you an answer that reflects the heart, soul and emotions of the other person, because it's based on their subjective feelings.

NATURAL SELLING® IS SELLING WITH SOUL

People skills are critical to your success in selling your business opportunity (your solution). This is where *Natural Selling®* can help you! Natural Selling® is a proven method of communication and selling, drawn from universally based principles that will allow you to learn the necessary people skills and successfully apply them.

This book focuses on giving you a working understanding of both the emotional (personal) and the logical (factual) reasons as to why people change and what will internally motivate them to want to partner with you for the long term.

PROSPECTIVE PARTNER OR PROSPECT?

I use the term *Potential Partner* throughout this book to replace the *label* of 'Prospect.' There is a saying that goes, "When you label someone, you negate him or her." Calling people prospects implies your prospective partners are units of production for you to use to achieve your objectives. People pick up on this even though you might not be aware of it. Your words are an extension of your thoughts and they create an energy you carry with you and that people intuitively tune into. You can't escape this unless you change your thoughts!

If you want to create relationships with potential partners, then what you say matters. Be careful of what you think and what you say! I can remember during my early days of selling, talking with a close sales associate about a customer in unflattering terms. He asked me afterwards if I wanted to keep her as a customer. I enquired as to why he asked me that. His response was one that has always stayed with me. "Have you ever thought that you carry the energy of the words you speak, and that your customer will pick up on that?" You will discover more about this concept in later chapters, which address the 4 principles upon which this book is founded.

REVERSING THE TRADITIONAL SELLING PARADIGM

Natural Selling® reverses the 'traditional pyramid' (see the diagram below) that occurs in most classical sales techniques. The traditional techniques that focus on presenting, closing and objection handling, put the emphasis on you and what you want rather than learning about your potential partner and what they want.

These classical techniques are the core elements of traditional selling and, for the most part, can be uncomfortable for both distributors and the people they talk with. This way of communicating tends to be adversarial and confrontational, which is unnecessary when you can actually learn how to sit on the same side of the table as your potential partner from the first moment you connect!

Traditional Selling Pyramid

10% Build Rapport

20% Identify Needs

30% Presentations

40% Close

The Traditional Selling Pyramid illustrates the percentage of time in front of the potential partner using traditional selling strategies. The strategies focus only on presenting the distributor's interpretation of a solution, not on understanding the logical and emotional needs of the potential partner.

The Natural Selling® paradigm and pyramid in selling redistributes the communication components required and lowers the total time invested to get an agreement. This is accomplished by understanding your potential partner's problems, needs and wants so you can make a customized and therefore more effective presentation of your business opportunity as a solution. This understanding allows you to recognize a person's real motivation to change.

Natural Selling® Pyramid

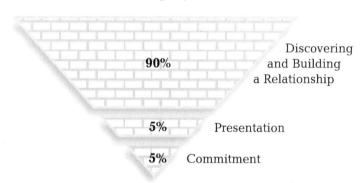

90% — Discovering and Building a Relationship

5% — Presentation

5% — Commitment

By inverting the old paradigm, you focus greater energy and more time on connecting and understanding the initial part of the sales process.

HOW DO YOU ACCOMPLISH THIS?

Natural Selling® is based on 4 Principles and the use of Dialogue to communicate. Dialogue has been mostly lost to the modern world and yet was used extensively and effectively by the ancient Greeks and many native Indian societies. Dialogue is perhaps *the* most powerful way of communicating that is available to you whether in selling or in everyday communication. Practice it with good intent and it will create an energy field of openness and understanding between you and your potential partners with the end result being more positive than you would normally anticipate.

The 4 Principles that form the foundation are:

1. Helping other people solve their problems.
2. Listening to what is being meant, not just what is being said.
3. Asking the right questions at the right time.
4. Feeding back what you think you heard they want.

You communicate this by using Dialogue – 'Heart-to-Heart' communication.

Dialogue is used within the five stages of a Conversation Framework:

1. Connecting
2. Discovering and Listening
3. Transitioning
4. Presenting
5. Committing and Supporting

If you choose to adopt the universal principle that your mission is to help others and thereby help yourself and expand your business, then selling your business opportunity/solution should be fun and profitable. You have an opportunity to earn more money than at any other time in your life and achieve a greater sense of fulfillment, while realizing your dreams for a better future. If you're not having fun and not on track for achieving your personal and income goals, work closely with your mentors to determine where you need help as you take the journey toward self-determination.

Remember, the roads you will take are for traveling, not for destinations!

How To Use This Book

*Your success will be as good
as the plan you make for yourself
to implement what you learn.*

I have written this book with the idea that many of the chapters can stand on their own. What this means to you is that you can start with any chapter and have an understanding of its content without having to read the previous chapters. Because of this there is some repetition. But as repetition is the mother of success . . . !

I have also opted to introduce the possible challenges and their causes you're possibly facing first; find out why they are happening and then talk about the solution after. This gives you a better understanding of why something might not be working for you so that you will know what to do to change it. It's also congruent with the way I suggest you talk with people. *Problems first – Solutions later!*

Seven Actions For Turning Theory Into Practice

1. Practice, Practice, Practice

Practice, practice, practice with real people all the time. Practice one thing at a time in small steps. Notice how people's attitudes toward you change as you progress. Observe others responding to you differently. Do it and be it! 'Doing' and 'Being' create changes. That will take a little time. You might be like that proverbial water faucet that hasn't been turned on for a while – it's going to be a little rusty at first, but it will work.

2. Quantity Of Practice Is More Important Than Quality

The quality and deeper understanding will follow. This is not a numbers game of 'How many people can you get through and present to in a day.' This is a numbers game of 'How many *quality problem-solving conversations* can you have in a day.' The only way you can get good is to do it. *Even as you start to take mini steps, you'll find you'll still be ahead of where you were. Just a 15% improvement can turn you into the star you already are!*

3. Keep Your Conversations Relaxed

It's not always what you ask or say, it's when you ask or say it. Keep your conversations, well . . . conversational. Don't let your enthusiasm overwhelm people.

Come from a point of really wanting to understand the other person. It all starts with you and your intent. Be interested in people and what they're about. They will feel this and you'll be amazed at how quickly most people will open up to you.

4. Let Go Of Your Attachment To The Outcome!

While you do have an agenda – regard it as a *conditional agenda*. This means your agenda only comes out when you know it's appropriate to talk about it; when you know the other person is open to looking for a change, and you believe your solution is the right one for them. Let your objectives guide you, as opposed to letting them manipulate the conversation. Keep the conversation open. *The outcome is a result of the integrity of the process.* It's the process that will create the relationship and, ultimately, the sale. *Let go of your outcome and your income will increase!*

5. Do Not Start 'Selling' As Soon As You 'Glimpse' An Opportunity!

You hear people say all the time, "I wish I had more money." Or, "The only way out as I see it, is to start my own business." How many times have you heard something like this and jumped in with your solution only to be disillusioned with a negative response? Most times this is *not* the time to jump in. Presenting too early is the number one cause of objections and rejection. Instead find out what is behind this kind of statement.

6. Go Slow To Go Fast!

Take time. Look at it as a 'journey of discovery.' The more time you invest in preparing, the easier it is to complete your journey. A Chinese proverb says, "Wait long and strike fast." It's like climbing a mountain – the higher you climb, the more you see and understand.

7. Invest Time In People

If you only find only one person a month, who joins you for the right reasons, and that person is prepared to do what is necessary to change their circumstances, and each person did the same thing, and so on, all within the same 12-month period, how many distributors would you have on your team at the end of the year? 4,096! That's 4,096 motivated distributors and customers doing the right things for the right reasons.

Here's the key. Find the *right* people who want to join with you. People who want to make a difference in their lives – just as you are doing. Your team will be strong, loyal and work with you for a lifetime!

Objectives Of The Book

The objectives of this book are to:

- Help you change your thoughts and your approach to 'selling' and business, so you can get the positive results you're seeking in less time, without using traditional presentational, persuasive or manipulative techniques.

- Eliminate whatever anxieties or fears you might have about connecting with people when approaching them about your business.

- Learn how to ask skillful, non-intrusive questions that allow people to think about, and reveal to you, as well as themselves, their real needs, and allow them to persuade themselves to join you.

- Learn how to listen to what people say and don't say, and what to listen for, that will motivate them to listen to you.

- Customize this communication to suit your own style and personality.

Part I

Chapter 1:
Introduction: A Personal History

Chapter 2:
The Cause Of Rejection!

Chapter 3:
4 Principles To Eliminate
The Cause Of Rejection!

CHAPTER 1

Introduction:
Believe Nothing!

Believe nothing merely because you have been told it.
Do not believe what your teacher tells you merely out of respect
for the teacher. But whatsoever, after due examination and analy-
sis, you find to be kind, conducive to the good, the benefit
the welfare of all beings – that doctrine believe and cling
to and take it as your guide. – Buddha

FROM THERE TO HERE

In 1979 when I entered the world of professional selling, I learned the techniques, the manipulative phrases, the strategies, the systems, and how to use persuasion, that was designed to make me successful. I bought books on closing and objection-handling techniques and how to negotiate to win. Within a year, I could handle up to seven objections and continually bridge to a close. The money flowed!

There were two problems though. The tension and the anxiety that came with it was, at times, suffocating. Plus the money flowed out as fast as it was coming in.

Outwardly, when presenting, handling objections and closing all the time, I looked calm. However, if you had observed closely you would have noticed one arm trailing down the back of the chair I was sitting on fiercely gripping the leg of the chair to relieve the tension that was inside me.

So why was the tension there? Though I didn't know it at the time, the reason was because I felt I was treating people in a way that I would not like to be treated myself.

I stuck with it because I didn't know there was any other way of selling, and the sales profession was the closest thing to give me the freedom I was seeking. But the freedom came at a price. While I had the relative freedom, the money and being an independent salesperson gave me, my soul was compromised by what was an adversarial approach of using traditional sales techniques to get it. As I didn't know any other way, I accepted that way as a truth.

I saw others being successful at using the traditional approach as well. Many were more successful than me, and appeared comfortable doing the same thing. This added to my dilemma. I felt there must be something wrong with me if I couldn't accept the techniques and the systems as easily as they could. You might find yourself feeling the same thing.

MIXED MESSAGES!

The inner conflict I was experiencing stemmed from the mixed messages that classical sales training invokes. No matter how the sales training manuals cloaked it with their words about serving the potential customer, in reality it was all about serving the bottom line and profits. Nothing wrong with the bottom line – as Peter Ueberroth, who led the 1984 Olympics in Los Angeles said, "Be proud of profits, for without profits, there is no growth and, without growth, there is no vitality."

But taking a Machiavellian approach that the "End justifies the means" was hard to accept. An illustration of this is when I re-read recently a 'principle' while thumbing through a well-known sales training book I had used. "Don't give people a chance to think, or the answers they come up with may not be the ones you want." This one sentence speaks volumes about manipulation! It makes me shudder to think I had accepted this as being the right way.

Because of training like this, most people think that selling is all about the art and science of manipulation as demonstrated via the media, television programs, newspapers and books. And they are right! Modern techniques of manipulative persuasion have distorted the true essence of selling which is to be of service. Most of us have first-hand experiences of this manipulation from salespeople we allow to persuade us into buying something we don't want: from salespeople who don't listen or bother to find out what we are really asking; and, from salespeople who respond to our questions based on what they want to tell us.

BUILT-IN CONFUSION

Unfortunately, today's sales training methods haven't changed much in that the message is still mixed. While they still start by teaching you how to find needs, they then regress into teaching techniques of how to ask manipulative questions, how to 'close' the sale and how to 'handle objections' in the event that the 'prospect' might not be co-operative and show some resistance. No wonder many distributors and salespeople get confused and anxious when it comes to selling. The process is one of contradiction!

The tragedy of this is that a distributor's focus is not on finding out what a person wants, why they want it and then providing it for them. Instead, the distributor's thoughts and words are focused on how to handle the objections they have been told will come up when they close, and thinking of techniques of how to squash the objections, and how to deal with the rejection that is surely to be there. Well, guess what? If you're focusing on what you don't want, that's what you're going to get. What you don't want. Period. It's the law of Cause and Effect kicking in as night follows day. Be careful of thoughts because they have a habit of coming true!

To me, selling like this is contradictory, incongruent and a complete oxymoron! Not only that, it pits people against people.

DISTRIBUTORS WON'T DO IT!

Most distributors know all this! They have been on the receiving end of this type of behavior and don't feel comfortable with the notion of selling. They have come to understand it from their own experiences. That is why many of them won't go out and sell or even entertain the notion of selling when the idea of becoming a distributor is introduced!

MONEY AND HOW YOU EARN IT?

Using techniques in my early years of selling fed another hidden subconscious factor that worked against me. I couldn't hang on to the money I was making. I never fully enjoyed it. There was something missing.

I discovered later the money felt tainted because the techniques I was using were in conflict with my soul. Subconsciously I felt the money, which was supposed to be the reward for my actions, was deceitfully obtained. While I accepted the sales training I was given as the truth, at the same time it caused inner turmoil. While it is a truth, truths come in different forms if we are open to seeing them. I didn't see the 'other truths' at the time!

So, while the money came in, my own actions fulfilled the prophecy of the many myths that most of us are brought up on regarding money. "Money is the root of all evil." "Money isn't everything," making money is like, "Selling your soul to the devil . . . ." and so on. I wasn't able to intellectualize it. It was a feeling, and feelings in our Western Society where logic prevails don't count for much. So intellectual guidance for feelings was hard to come by.

If you find you have the same issues over the money in your business, this might strike a chord!

Now that's all changed. By discovering that selling and integrity are quite natural partners, I can now gratefully receive and keep the abundant rewards that daily come my way. The pie of abundance is unlimited. The pie is infinite. Making money does not mean someone has to win and someone has to lose. It's a natural exchange. If you're of service, expect to get paid for it, and everyone is better off.

Seek And You Shall Find!

Eventually, after a few years of using the classical style of selling, I went to a friend who was a successful sales manager, and explained my dilemma. His response was to tell me that selling is like acting. "Like an actor, you put on your selling costume and go out onto the stage of the business world. Like an actor you learn your lines and how to deliver them. Like an actor, you deliver your lines with emotion so as to seduce the audience and persuade them into a different state. Like an actor, you put on a 'face' that hides the real you from yourself and others so as to do the job." Besides, he added, "It's good for you, your family and the country!" That's what he said, almost word for word.

His answer didn't work for me. It was unsatisfactory for someone who was seeking some enlightenment. I didn't want to be an 'actor.' I wanted to be 'me,' even though 'me' was growing and, by all accounts, had a long way to go! I felt there had to be another way. There was! *What we seek is always there in front of us. The first step on any journey to find it is a thought – an intention.*

The Universe in its wisdom is kind. When the intention is put into the universe, (the "infinite organizing power" according to Deepak Chopra), it places in front of you the course to take, if you allow yourself to see, choose and take it. It's like buying a new car. Once you have set your mind on the make and the color, have you noticed that suddenly you see them all over the place? The truth is, they were always there. We just had never focused on them before!

So by being open myself, I found the first of many doors beginning to open. The first was a door to a counselor form of selling, a method based on asking questions. I learned to ask questions and got to understand more. I still presented a lot on the front end of meetings, but I also asked a lot more questions; questions that gave me a better picture of the other person;

questions however that ironically enabled me to use my manipulative skills more effectively at the time.

For example, a question I used to start most sales presentations went like this, *"Before I start talking about my products Mr./Mrs. Buyer, let's focus on you and find out what you're looking for, for example . . . ."* and I would ask a series of prepared leading questions that 'self-served' me to the sale.

I still ask the same thing today (this is still a great way to start a conversation), but the intent is different. It's the *intent* behind the question that is really important. People *feel* intent. Those distributors who embrace a similar humanistic or more soulful behavior toward their potential customers win, hands down. This is not esoteric stuff! Eminent empirical evidence such as the Lominger Studies and books like HeartMath prove this.

For example, it's proven that the heart is an organ that has feelings that affect the rest of the body. If you yell at someone or treat them in an adversarial way, it can take up to eight hours for the heart and the rest of the body to settle down into a normal peaceful productive rate again. The heart knows, and two hearts connected in harmony can go a lot further than two heads disconnected by being in conflict.

By the way, don't throw away everything you learned in the old school of selling if you were brought up that way; 85% of it is still useable. Just change the intent!

TECHNIQUES ARE STILL TECHNIQUES

So while my ability to understand where people were coming from, and my ability to make money increased, my discomfort still remained.

The problem was that the new techniques were still techniques. They'd just been moved around. My focus was still on getting the sale. *The techniques didn't seem to have any philosophical foundation that went deeper than the logic on which they were built.* They were built on quicksand, forever shifting, and they still treated people as if they were objects of which to take advantage.

Occasionally, it would affect my sales activity. I would find other things to do, rather than face going out and finding new customers or follow up on calls. My comfort level at best only improved marginally.

A 2 A.M. Wake Up Call!

Then one morning I woke up about 2 A.M. and asked myself a question: What if I really believed that first statement about wanting to focus on and serve the other person? What if I believed it so much I was prepared to give up the manipulative approach, and to really listen to what my prospective client was saying, and was really prepared to let the sale go if I determined my solution could not meet their needs? Not only that. What if I was even prepared to suggest an alternative solution if I knew where there was one? I decided to let it happen and went back to sleep.

It Happened!

Well, the universe can be perverse as well as kind, and it took a while for a situation to come up. Two months in fact! The time between the 2 A.M. resolution and happenstance was long enough for me to have consciously forgotten about it. Yet, subconsciously, it was sitting there, like water under the ground, waiting for the right moment to be a spring.

So two months later, sitting opposite a prospective client, I was staring my 2 A.M. question and resolution in the face. We had come to a point in the conversation where I realized my solution was okay but not what the client was looking for. I also realized I was facing my own shadow. The devil on my right shoulder urged me to go for the sale. "A little bit of persuasive talk here and there, and it's in the bag. Remember your responsibility to your company and to your family, go on, go for it." On my left was another voice saying very quietly in a sing-song voice, "Remember your promise to yourself."

It was hard. Years of ingrained habits and experience are not easy to remove. I decided to go with the 2 A.M. commitment, and said I didn't feel I had the right solution. On being asked to explain why, I gave the reason based on what I had heard.

And then the first of two most extraordinary things happened. The first was that the person I was talking with leaned forward and asked what he could do to adjust the company's criteria so as to use my solution. The inner conflict bounced back, grounded from years of habitual use. The two opposing voices sprung up again, one wanting to grab the opportunity, the other reminding me of my commitment. It was a massive internal struggle. I went for the 2 A.M. commitment and stated again, that based on what they had told me, my solution was not going to be satisfactory for them, and left!

The second extraordinary thing was how this action was later returned in abundance. It came back in the form of two contracts from people I had not approached before. One of them was from an unsolicited referral given by the very person I could not help. In terms of the spirit, though I did not know it then, I had detached myself from the outcome – and my income had increased! The outcome can manifest itself in many ways. You have to be open to see it.

What also increased was my comfort level, self-esteem, understanding and the beginning of inner peace. *There is strength in being open to the vulnerability of letting go.* It was also the continuation of a journey that finds me today still questioning and sometimes overturning conventional practices and discovering there are other 'truths,' especially when these truths are anchored by ancient philosophies that can answer all our questions. In fact, I now look for the contradictions in life because, for me invariably, the contradiction is where the truth is. It's usually where the opportunity is as well.

Seeing the truth in a contradiction can reveal that things are not what they always seem. As a simple example, why do we call modern medicine – 'traditional' medicine? It's not traditional, it's relatively modern and based on curing the disease and using mostly artificial means to do it. The real traditional medicine is based on the ancient wisdoms of herbs and natural substances to prevent and cure ailments. The same traditions and substances, by the way, that we destroy on a daily basis in the name of advancement, which make us more dependent on these artificial technologies.

While we're on the subject, here is another contradiction. Why do we use the term 'Traditional Selling' when it's not? It, too, is comparatively modern as a product of the Madison Avenue advertising agencies. Perhaps we might want to call it Modern Selling?

SELLING – THE 'OTHER' TRUTH

The truth for me now is that traditional sales system based on techniques, is no longer my truth. There is no judgment here. If it works for you and you are comfortable with it, that's fine. In the words of Hans-Peter Durr, a 77-years young German quantum physicist, "This is not an Either/Or world. This is an As Well world!"

The significance of the 'As Well' statement really hit home to me a few years ago while attending a convention. As a courtesy, I went to introduce myself to a distributor whom I had not met before though I had trained some of his downline.

He informed me he saw Natural Selling® in conflict with his own standard Network Marketing approach. I asked him what his training comprised of and discovered it was telling his story, giving away tapes, presenting to as many people as possible, and so on. The reason he saw it as a conflict was because his approach tended to be more left-brain, logical and factual, and Natural Selling® has to do more with communication and people skills – a right-brain, feeling and emotional activity.

Personally, I didn't see any conflict. It's just another option that if it works for you, then use it.

After talking about this apparent difference, we got to discussing the high attrition rate in Network Marketing, and I asked, "*Why is it do you think, that only 5% to 10% of distributors seem to succeed in this industry?*"

To which he replied, "It's the 20/80 rule!"

Most people have heard of the 20/80 rule. This is where it's said that 20% of the people do 80% of the business. It's a rule I have accepted for many years until I discovered another truth. Although I knew what the 20/80 was, I asked another question to find out *his* meaning: "*When you say the 20/80 rule, what do you mean by that?*"

"Well, you know, that's where 20% of the people do 80% of the business."

"*And what if,*" I asked, "*that was not entirely true? What if the reason that 20% of people do 80% of the business, is that the 20% made up the rules? Rules that don't work for the other 80%?*" I then added, "*What would happen if you gave the other 80% the option of using a different approach to use, an approach that allowed them to be just as successful, perhaps even more so?*"

Continuing, I suggested, "*And what if, only 10% of those 80% were successful? What would that do for your business?*" (It would nearly double, of course!)

With that I excused myself and left him to ponder the question, as he had as much right to his opinion as I did mine. Besides, 'telling' in a situation like this can be counterproductive. New thoughts are like wine, they need to mature before coming out of the bottle.

HOW TO SELL NETWORK MARKETING

13

We all live in our own truths. This is the significance of the meaning by Buddha at the start of this chapter when he said, "Believe nothing because you have merely been taught it." What he was saying was, "Do not even believe me." All our truths are based on our own experience, which is unique to us. I believe we live in an as well world and it can serve us to allow others the freedom to think what they like. Once the significance of this becomes a realization, anyone can chart his/her own course, free of the encumbrances of others, and succeed.

MAYBE IT'S YOUR TRUTH?

What if the reason you have difficulty getting the things you personally want in your life – love, money, freedom, health, peace, security, appreciation, acceptance and so on – is because y*ou allow* yourself to think and operate under rules that don't work for you? Just because these rules are successful for someone else, does it mean they will work for you? This can apply to everything just as it applies to sales.

What if you did things differently? What if you knew how to march to the beat of your own drum and easily found what you were looking for?

If your own inner peace, and that of the world, is important to you as an individual and collectively for the world, *what if* you replaced the 'either/or' approach with an 'as well' approach? What if instead of saying to your downline, "Do it my way because it worked for me," you said, instead, *"This way worked for me, let's see if it will do the same thing for you and, if not, let's seek an alternative!"* What if . . . ?

PROSPERITY YOUR DIVINE RIGHT!

When I first started selling I saw this sticker on a car's bumper. It read, 'Prosperity Your Divine Right!' I used to laugh and ridicule it, because it was a truth I did not see and understand. Now I smile and think, "How true!" Prosperity is our divine right if we individually choose to take it. It's right up there with happiness and everything else we would like. It's just that since birth, we have allowed society, our peers, our parents, our teachers, our religions, our institutions and our governments to interpret how we should think and do things, by infiltrating and influencing our feelings, thoughts, words and actions. That includes the way we think about money and what we think about selling. It's up to us to change.

THE PRESENT

For me the inner peace in selling and in life continues. I still use most of the words and phrases I used when I first started selling – the difference being, they now have a foundation and a different intent: A philosophic and principled foundation.

Natural Selling® is not new. It's an approach based on centuries-old wisdoms and methods. It's been around for a long time and it can work for everyone. Modern-day research proves this, notwithstanding the fact that 95% of distributors can't be wrong.

Besides, you can discover this for yourself by taking your own Journey of Discovery. As you practice the things you learn in this book, heed once more the paraphrased words of Buddha, "Believe nothing merely because you have been told it. Do not even believe me. Believe what you believe to be the truth for you. Once you have discovered it, embrace it and take it as your guide!"

Different thinking, different doing, and different being reveal different truths. I hope you find the truth that is within you!

CHAPTER 2

The Cause Of Rejection!

Today's customer wants to be understood, not talked at!

Have you considered that if you get anxious about meeting people and it prevents you from talking with them, or you feel the need to get pumped up before you meet your prospective customers, or you drag your feet before making those calls, it could be it's the way you are communicating, or think you have to communicate, that is causing this problem?

Ask yourself this. What is the greatest fear you, and other distributors in your downline have, that holds you back from talking with people about your business, products or services? Is it the fear of Rejection?

And how does it make you feel when you get rejected? Tense? Feeling worthless – lowered self-esteem? A wrench in the stomach?

It's not so much what happens to me as what happens in me!

Stiffening in the neck? It's different feelings for different people. And they're real feelings, aren't they? *It's not so much what happens to me as what happens in me!*

TWO TYPES OF REJECTION

In my experience there are two kinds of rejection: the flat in your face 'Not Interested' type of rejection, and the type where someone has looked at your solution and finds it really doesn't fit what they need. The second one can be disappointing but it doesn't necessarily feel personal. So I'm addressing the first one!

You have probably been told that rejection is part of selling and to learn to expect it, to deal with it, to get over it, and that it's a numbers game of getting as many 'No' answers that will get you closer to 'Yes' answers. And you might even have learned how to do that.

Well, I'll share with you that I believe it's nonsense! I don't subscribe to that kind of thinking and training because you can eliminate rejection – not by mind games or mental tricks – but by eliminating the cause of it!

The Cause Of Rejection!

Let's look at the cause of rejection, because before we can start looking at Natural Selling® as a possible solution, would you agree that it's important to explore and identify the cause of your problem first? Why is this? Well, doesn't it make sense that coming from a place of understanding of what is causing this problem called rejection will give you a better idea as to what you can do to about it?

And yet, isn't it true that most distributors bring up their solutions, or tell people how they can help them, far too early in their conversations, and then what happens? They get rejected!

So if you do get rejected . . . who causes it? You do!

In our Western, fast-paced culture, we create the problem of rejection for ourselves with our quick band-aid solutions to everything because we don't explore what is behind people's needs. We don't spend time even finding out whether someone's problem really is a problem and what is causing it.

We all have our opinions and answers about things and we all think ours is the right one for everyone else. We quickly come up with our solutions to others' problems as we interpret them based on our own experiences. We are very 'solution oriented' in this society. The problem with providing a quick solution without finding the history of a problem is that we are in danger of offering the wrong solution or even unconsciously offending people because we haven't involved them in the conversation.

For example, you hear the following statement in its many different forms, "I wish I had more money." or, "I wish my health was better." How do most network marketers normally respond? Usually with an "I can show you how . . ." or "You know what you should do . . . ." response.

Lack of money, lack of health, lack of anything, is not usually the problem. It's the symptom of the problem. The real problem is what is causing the lack of money or lack of health. That is what you need to explore, and very few distributors do this and involve the people they talk with. They prefer to tell and if you find yourself doing the same thing you can make the choice to part company with this kind of behavior and in doing so change the results you're presently getting.

A DOCTOR ANALOGY

If you went to a doctor and complained of a pain in your shoulder, and without asking any questions or even examining you, he/she wrote a prescription and told you to go to the pharmacy for some drugs, how would you feel about the doctor? Probably not very convinced, and you almost certainly would not fill the prescription. The reason is that the doctor did not involve you in the process.

You will be doing the same thing if you present your business opportunity as a solution too early. When you tell someone about what you have, and how they should do it because it will improve their lives, and not only that, you've got the best compensation plan and the best this, and the best that, and you know it's going to be good for them – whose point of view does it appear to the other person that you're focusing on? Yours!

When you *are* fortunate enough to finally find someone to listen to you and when they ask questions and you respond by treating their questions as objections with, "Yes, but . . . ." answers, whose agenda does it appear you are focusing on? Yours again! And, how about when you use 'closing techniques,' whose agenda and whose point of view are you focusing on? Yours!

Are people interested in your agenda or what you think, or what you think they should do? Mostly not – even when you have their best interests at heart. How many times have you seen someone close to you in great need of your business opportunity or products and they won't listen to you because you told them what they should do?

Most people are not interested in being told or persuaded you have the right answer for them. Even if they asked you! I have spoken with thousands of distributors about this. Distributors who are frustrated because they believe their products can help, and sometimes save a life, but they just can't get the other person's attention.

Why is that? Well, it appears that the very thing distributors want other people to do, which is to *listen* to them, *is the very thing they don't do themselves!* They spend too much time attempting to tell and convince and not enough time asking questions and listening. Letting our need to tell and master others keeps us from discovering the truth. Using the ancient wisdom from Lao Tzu, we are reminded that, *"Mastering others is force. Mastering yourself is true power."*

The truth is, it doesn't matter what you think about your product or your solutions. It's what the other person thinks. And, if you start your conversations overpowering people and telling them what they should do, most will withdraw – *'People love to buy, but hate to be sold.'* People are looking for more meaning and understanding before you start proposing your solutions.

Observe your own experiences. Have you ever been in a situation where you asked someone for a solution to a problem and they perhaps started with the words, "You know what you should do . . . ." and then rattled off their answer? Did you feel a little resentful or annoyed? It's probably because you didn't feel involved and your own uniqueness was not being acknowledged. As human beings there is one thing we all have in common – we are all different. We need to recognize, embrace and understand that difference.

If people are not interested in you and what you think, then whom are they interested in? Themselves! So if you begin with presenting your prospective partners information, or tell them what you think is best for them, or tell them all about you, without finding out much about them, they can get defensive because they hear it as you telling them what's right for them, and they feel manipulated and get turned off.

> *Today's customer does not want to be talked at or told – today's customer wants to be asked and heard.*

And that is why you get rejected. And, incidentally, why you get objections as well! So, if you get worn out with the rejection and objections you create, and don't feel inspired to talk with people, now you have a possible explanation as to why. *Today's customer does not want to be talked at or told – today's customer wants to be asked and heard.*

PEOPLE WILL NO LONGER BE TOLD

Winston Churchill, in one of his many eloquent moments, said, "Personally I'm always ready to learn, although I do not always like being taught."

Because we have all this knowledge about our businesses, products and services we think that the only way to get this knowledge over to the other person is to use a fire hose presentation and tell them. Your knowledge can be an asset that gets in your way! In the words of Mark Van Doren, "The art of teaching is the art of assisting discovery." Or, as my meditation coach, Francis Warner puts it, "The idea is not to teach something, but to remind each other what we already know!" You will learn this art and learn how to use your knowledge and teach others in a different way – a precise way. A way that creates a willing environment for people to learn, by turning your statements into questions that allow others to participate.

These are not just my findings and just my experiences. The research and the data are in. According to studies done by the Huthwaite group, a major behavioral training organization, it's shown that the majority of the world's population won't use these sales techniques and don't like them being used on them. People today are more, knowledgeable, demanding, skeptical, educated, have higher expectations, control the buying power, have *been there, done that,* and their kids have gone through the same thing as well.

If you want people to understand you and your ideas, understand them and where they are coming from, and what is happening in their lives and how it's affecting them first.

The good news is that there is an alternative to all this telling!

CHAPTER 3

4 Principles
To Eliminate The Cause
Of Rejection!

Involve me and I will understand.
– Ancient Chinese proverb

If you knew how to talk with anyone – strangers, business associates, best friends, anyone – about your business, and never had to say much about who you are, or what you're doing unless you were asked and, during the conversation, you could discover one or all of the following:

- You would know precisely where the person you're talking with is coming from, (who they are, their inner values, what they want, why they want it, what they don't want, why they don't want it, and so on), and what their problems were if they had any.

- You would know whether they wanted to change their present situation. The majority will. You would also know whether they were ready to change and hear what you have to offer.

- And, when you presented your solution, you would know precisely what to say that would interest them in looking closely at your business opportunity.

If all that could happen, do you think talking with people, making and returning telephone calls would be anxiety free and that your success would soar? Of course it would!

You can do that. It's very much within you to do so. If it's not happening for you already, it requires you to do something. You have to change.

CHANGE THE WAY YOU THINK AND DO THINGS!

Changing two things – the way you *think* and the way you *communicate* – can achieve for you the success you're looking for without the anxiety normally associated with selling! You can bring harmony into your life, and the lives of others, by learning how to communicate with people in a way that assures every conversation you have will end with something positive.

It could be an agreement to partner, an agreement to continue the conversation, unsolicited referrals or perhaps just a conversation that leaves the other person feeling good about you and Network Marketing. There are any number of possibilities.

TETHERED MINDS

Over time we allow ourselves to get trapped with certain ways of thinking. The story, "Tethered With The Reed Of a Lotus Flower" in a book by Mary Morrissey, called, *Building Your Field of Dreams* illustrates just how limiting our beliefs can sometimes be. In India, when a young elephant is born to a working elephant, its freedom to roam is limited by having one end of a chain fastened to its leg and the other end tethered to a tree. The elephant learns quite quickly that it can't get very far. As it gets older, the chain is substituted with a reed – a lightweight reed that it could easily break. But, because it can feel the reed around its ankle, it doesn't even try – the elephant is immobilized – it has subjugated itself.

It's not circumstances but choice that determines your present and your future!

The question is: What immobilizes the elephant? Is it the reed or its mind? It's its own mind! The philosopher, Yogi Amrit Desai, said, "Whatever you carry within you – you meet everywhere." The truth is that things don't happen to you, they happen because you let them happen. *It's not circumstances but choice that determines your present and your future!*

What you say, and how you act, is a result of your feelings and your thoughts. Change your thoughts and your words will change. Change your words and you will change the way people will respond to you. You *can* make this change immediately by just having the *intention* to do so, and keeping your mind free and finding your own truth. As the Bible says, 'The truth will set you free' but first it might upset you! Perhaps Natural Selling® is your truth.

NATURAL SELLING® - PRINCIPLED-BASED COMMUNICATION!

Natural Selling® is based on 4 Principles and uses a process of communicating called Dialogue. In chapter 5 you will learn more about how the use of Dialogue will draw people to you. You can apply this process to any relationship, be it business, family, friends or even in conflict resolution. Its application is universal. Dialogue will allow you to relate with people in a way that puts all the focus on others, from start to finish. The return on investment is that you get the things you want faster, without the negative feelings of rejection or anxiety because people will feel good about you and respond to you differently.

Natural Selling® is not a technique, or a something that fits the times of today. It is a way of communicating that's been with us for a long time – it will stay with us forever. It goes far beyond just selling – it's the essence of building relationships – whether it's with people you know, or don't know. It's where the 'R' word 'Rejection,' is replaced with the 'R' word 'Relationship.' It will change people's attitude to you. It will attract people to you. In fact, it's no different than having an ordinary conversation, except it will be skilled conversation.

Using techniques in communication can be transient. They can work for one person and not another. You might have seen or experienced the phenomena where a salesperson has been successful in one industry and, when moving to another industry, suddenly fails. One of the major reasons is that the sales techniques learned so effectively in the first industry were not transferable to another. It's like putting a round peg into a square hole. On the other hand, principled-based communication can be transferred. And methods based on principles can mostly be transferred as well.

THE 4 PRINCIPLES OF NATURAL SELLING®

So for the remainder of this chapter we'll look at the founding principles and philosophy behind Natural Selling®. Once the philosophy of something is grasped, it's easy to attach the mechanics to it. This is illustrated by the poem:

> *Techniques are many,*
> *Principles are few.*
> *Techniques will vary,*
> *Principles never do!*

PRINCIPLE #1: HELPING OTHER PEOPLE
SOLVE THEIR PROBLEMS

In my TeleClasses and Workshops I like to ask the question: *"What's the purpose of a business? Any business in the world? It doesn't matter what it is, or where it is. What is the purpose of a business? Or, why are you in business?"*

Most people will reply with something like, "To make a profit" or "Make money" or for "Self fulfillment." If you answered in this way, then ask yourself this: "On whom was your answer focused? – You or your potential customers?" It was on you, of course – you and your personal objective.

However, the fact is, you're not in business for you. You're in it for other people. The *purpose* of a business is simply to help other people solve their problems. If you're wondering about this, ask yourself this question. If your product or service cannot solve someone's problems, is there any reason for them to do business with you?

So it's all about the other person and it's all to do with problem solving isn't it? As distributors and salespeople we are, in fact, *problem solvers*. Spend your waking hours looking for problems, for with problems comes opportunity. *In essence, another person's problem becomes both your and their opportunity!*

The Chinese recognize this duality of thought by using the combined symbols for crisis, which is Danger and Opportunity. The Eastern Philosophies once more appear to provide for us much of the foundation of what we need in Western Culture.

wei
-Danger
-Peril
-Hazard

Looking at this more closely, the question, "What's in it for me?" is the internal dialogue of the ego! Focusing on your ego has a tendency to prevent you

chi
-Opportunity
-The moving
  power

from getting what you want. Asking the question, *"How can I help?"* is the dialogue of the spirit. Focusing and taking action on your spirit will bring you the abundance you desire. If you're presently focused on your ego, (what's in it for me?) exchange the energy of your present thoughts, words and actions, for a different energy – an energy of how you can help. Make sure it's not an energy of persuading the other person even if you find them in great need. Allow them to persuade themselves and take responsibility for their own actions. You'll find that when you change, the responses you get will change also.

Doing this effectively and focusing on your purpose of helping other people solve their problems, *will achieve for you your objective* – which is whatever your own reason for being in business is. Don't ignore your objective. Let it be satisfied at the right time after you have discovered what both of you need to know to make a decision. Deep down we all have our own special reasons for wanting to do what we do that is unique to ourselves and we must not forget to have our desires satisfied as well, so as to maintain balance in our lives.

INTENT

It's important to really accept this. Absorb this mindful 'act of service' into your being. If you embrace this cornerstone principle and make this your purpose, your intent in life, you will immediately tap into universal laws of attraction. In Deepak Chopra's book, *The Seven Spiritual Laws of Success,* he talks about the 7th Law – the Law of Purpose in life. By focusing on your purpose and by knowing how to manifest it into physical reality, you will have the key to the door of success and abundance that you're seeking.

Your anxiety about calling people will be eliminated as well. That telephone at the end of your desk – the one that weighs 20 lbs. in the mornings when you go to make your calls – will literally float into your hands. There is nothing like making calls to people who are eagerly waiting for you. So, pay attention to your purpose and pay attention in putting your objective aside until the time is right to bring it up! *Let go of the outcome and your income will increase.*

So, how do you find out if people have the sort of problems you can help them solve? You ask simple questions, you listen and you respond to the answers!

PRINCIPLE #2: LISTENING TO WHAT IS BEING MEANT, NOT JUST WHAT IS BEING SAID

More than anything else, I know, the mere act of listening will draw people to you like a magnet. Remove your ego and the necessity to randomly talk about you and your solutions in your sales conversations, and you will achieve more than you can ever imagine.

Do we listen to people? Based on my experience, we don't. And we appear to listen least to those we are closest to, and understand them the least as well! And here is the other side of this coin. They don't listen to us either. The reasons for this are numerous and beyond the scope of this book.

This is how we normally listen – 45% of the time we are supposed to be listening, we are working out what we're going to say next. Another 45% of the time is spent waiting for a gap in the conversation so we can say it – leaving only 10% of the time listening. So, are we listening when we spend only 10 % of the time doing it? No! We can't be. So, how much of the time should we spend listening? 100%! (When I ask this question, most of the responses I get are from 60% to 95%. The reason being, of course, is that people think they need to reserve some space to think about what they will say or ask next.)

Hearing and listening 100% requires you to do something that is alien for most people, because they are never taught it. It requires you to let go of your need to clutter your mind with needless thoughts of working out what to say next, and to let the inner self take over. It requires you to listen and tap into to the essence of the other person. It requires you to listen to the other 90% that you normally miss, because that's where the real information is and how the relationship is cemented.

So how do you listen 100% of the time? Here are a few clues: First, you have the ability to think 10 times faster than anyone can talk. If you know something about your business opportunity or products, and you listen to what is behind the problems revealed to you, you will automatically connect what they want with the *correct* features of your solution. Later, you can use those features to solve the problems you have heard. It's like having the features of your business opportunity stored in lots of spring-loaded drawers in the back of your mind, like the compact disc drawer on your computer. The right drawers with the right features will automatically pop out to solve the specific problems you hear. If, you hear them!

YOUR QUESTIONS COME FROM THE ANSWERS!

Another clue about being able to listen 100% is that *what you're going to say next is in the answers you get to your previ-*

ous questions! It's all there! It's just that you must listen to the answers. Most distributors and salespeople listen selectively – listening for the things they want to hear – if they listen at all.

They listen with the intent to reply, not with the intent to understand the facts and feelings of where someone is coming from. Real listening requires letting go and concentrating on everything the other person says and doesn't say. If you think about it, it makes sense. People know the history of their life, and if you are to have any success in understanding whether you can help them, doesn't it make sense to enlist their help by asking about it first, then listening and finally speaking?

A third clue is to stop re-interpreting what people say to you, based on your own life's experiences, judgments, prejudices and thoughts. For example, have you ever had someone respond to a remark you made and his or her response had no bearing on what you were talking about or what you were meaning? How did you feel about that? – Annoyed, unheard, invalidated, or some other feeling? What wasn't this person doing? They weren't listening! Do you probably do the same thing to others? In selling or in any communication, misunder-standings of this sort are expensive – expensive in terms of money and time and, more importantly, in terms of relationships.

> *There is a saying that goes: I know you believe you understand what you think I said. But I'm not sure you realize that what you heard is not what I meant!*

A classic story illustrates how we think we know what someone means when in fact we don't. A lady was talking with a friend of hers, and she was relating how her husband had left her the week before and she hadn't heard from him since. She had no idea where he was. Her friend replied, "Oh! I'm sorry to hear that, it must be awful for you!" "On the contrary," was the response, "I've been wondering how to get rid of him for ages!"

You see how our own thoughts can misinterpret someone's words and what they are meaning. If, in the above case, the friend had got behind the statement and asked, *"How do you feel about that?"* or, *"Tell me what happened,"* she would have had a clearer understanding of her feelings about the matter and would not have stepped into the minefield of miscommunication.

WE ARE ALL DIFFERENT!

Imagine you and everyone else in this world wearing different colored sunglasses. Would everything you see be the same as what everyone else sees? No. You might look at the same tree, for example, and yet its color would be different. This is true in the world. All of us see or imagine things differently.

It's the same with our thoughts and words. If I say the word 'blue,' you will have in your mind a shade of the color blue. I guarantee the shade of blue you have in your mind is not the same shade as what I'm thinking. The number of different shades of blue is infinite. One of your goals is to work out the color tint of the sunglasses of the person you're talking with. *Take time to look through another person's sunglasses before you assume you know the answers to their problem!*

CHANGING YOUR LISTENING HABITS

One of the challenges about effective listening is that (1) we're not sure how to listen, (2) what to listen for, or (3) even know how to respond to what someone says. From an early stage in our lives, what are we taught the most to get on in life – how to listen or how to express ourselves? Mostly, how to express ourselves!

The cruel truth is, the real art of communication is in the listening! Listening is a gift you can give anyone and it doesn't cost you a penny. Not only that, what you get in return is infinite. Deepak Chopra's book, *The Seven Spiritual Laws of Success*, states that, "The act of listening is one way to manifest the second law which is the Law of Giving." Interestingly, in my experience, this one action of listening will trigger all the other laws of success, turning them from a metaphysical reality into practical abundant reality.

There are two components to listening: understanding *how to listen, and what to listen for!* In subsequent chapters you'll learn how to actively listen, what to listen for, and understand where a person is coming from so that you can accurately propose your solution in words and meaning that the other person can relate to.

PRINCIPLE #3: HOW TO ASK THE RIGHT QUESTIONS AT THE RIGHT TIME

The true essence of selling, contrary to what you might have read in books, seen on television, and possibly have been used on you, is not about presenting, convincing, persuading, manipulating, or pushing someone to buy something.

You learned in chapter 2, that whenever you start off by telling people about you, your company, your products – especially early in your meeting – you are more than likely to cause the response of rejection and objections. It's the law of Cause and Effect working against you. It's crazy! When you use techniques that create the barriers of rejection and objections, you then have to learn more techniques to get over them. It never made sense to me.

MANIPULATIVE QUESTIONS GET SHORT-TERM RESULTS!

Manipulative questions can be very powerful. They are used to externally motivate someone into action. The end result is usually one of later regrets. And that's the Achilles Heel of the traditional selling approach. External motivation is used. The question is, can you externally motivate people? The answer is 'yes' you can; however it tends to wear off very quickly. It lends credence to the saying: *'A man convinced against his will is of the same opinion still.'*

The reason is that if you use manipulative questions, whose answers are you likely to receive? Yours or the person you're talking with? Yours mostly! And, while you can make people temporarily motivated to do something, what can happen after a short while? They stop being motivated. They stop doing what they agreed to do.

This later regret is a psychological behavior called buyers' remorse and you might see evidence of this in your downline where your distributors don't stay on the product or don't stay the course in your team. This is because they came on board for the wrong reasons. Your reasons, not theirs!

It's important to understand that any form of manipulation, whether you're doing it for you or doing it for them, is manipulation. People sense this and will enter into an agreement reluctantly.

Manipulative questions will get the answers you want, but will they get the answers you need?

Companies and advertising agencies put an amazing amount of energy and money towards keeping buyers' remorse to the minimum. For example, take those dazzling advertisements in magazines that advertise expensive cars. They are geared just as much to reassure the purchaser after the sale has been made, as they are to attract new buyers. Have you ever noticed being drawn to certain ads after you've made an expensive purchase to reassure yourself that you made the right decision?

Manipulative questions can conflict with the souls of others. People know, even though they allow themselves to be drawn in. You might have had manipulative questions used on you. If you have, how did it make you feel? Probably not so good, and you probably don't feel inclined to do this to others! *Manipulative questions will get the answers you want, but will they get the answers you need?*

NATURAL SELLING® QUESTIONS
REVEAL THE INNER TRUTH

In Natural Selling®, when I refer to 'questions,' I'm not referring to questions that are designed to get people to say what you want them to say. The questions I'm referring to are *principled questions* intended to bring out each person's *inner and external truth and values.* It's them talking about them, to you. After all, who has the history of what is, and has been, going on in their life? They do! Your potential partner and you each bring a key thing to the communication process.

On one hand, your potential clients have their history and know their needs. *They have the answers.* You, on the other hand, know the potential of your business opportunity to recognize whether specific aspects of it are going to work for them, and to be able to explain them in a way that makes complete sense. *So all you need are the right questions!*

You also need to know when to ask them. As you progress through this book, you will learn proven, non-intrusive, non-intimidating questions, which have different emotional powers: some have zero, some have a lot. You will learn how these questions are in a structure: what they are and when to use them to help you and the people you talk with see clearly where they are in the present; reveal whether they have any problems; and, if they do, whether the problems are important enough for them to want to do something about it.

Your questions help people open their minds. Questions involve people. They allow people to think about their lives, themselves and their problems.

HELP PEOPLE PERSUADE THEMSELVES

It's not about you persuading them – an approach that usually ends up with you owning the problem and the solution – it's about people persuading themselves. As people listen to themselves answer your questions they process the information internally as they are talking. Their answers help them think about their problems and to own the idea that they want to change if their problems and internal motivation is great enough.

> *When I say it, they can doubt me. When they say it, it's true.*

It gives meaning to the saying: "When I say it, they can doubt me. When they say it, it's true."

As people consciously and sub-consciously internalize what they are saying, their answers help them look at and challenge their beliefs as to why they allow their present situation to be as it is. And, depending on the degree of frustration they have with where they are, they start thinking about doing something to change it. Remember: *Your questions are for the other person as much as they are for you!* Or, to paraphrase the late John F. Kennedy, "Ask not what your questions will do for you. Ask what your questions will do for the other person."

So later in your conversation, after you have listened, and you suggest you might know of a solution that could take care of all their wants and needs, do you think most people will be open to listening to you? Yes, they will! Something interesting happens during these types of conversation – people like you –

you become their kind of person, because for the first time in a long time, someone, (you) is genuinely interested in them and what they're looking for and not attempting to ram a solution down their throat. They feel your intent. It's called Trust.

Look again at the first principle – it has to do with coming from a place of intent. You resonate this, and people pick up on it. Have you ever felt yourself being drawn closer to a person, and opened up to them because you felt they were really interested in you? After all, who is the most fascinating person in the world? You are! And you're not alone. Everyone feels the same way about himself or herself.

Asking questions eliminates the need for you to present and to learn closing and objection-handling techniques, because who eliminates all the objections in the conversation? They do because they are the ones talking and revealing their problems to both you and themselves.

THE 'SALE' IS IN THE PROCESS!

Learning how to ask the right questions at the right time will prepare a person who is talking with you to be receptive to your solutions and, essentially, sell him/herself on the idea that you can help. The 'sale' is made not at the end with closing techniques and objection-handling skills – it's made during the process where both of you are discovering what your potential client or partner is looking for, and why they want

The degree that a person will change is mostly dependent on the degree of discomfort he/she is presently feeling.

it. Remember: *The degree that a person will change is mostly dependent on the degree of discomfort he/she is feeling with their present situation.*

If the person you're talking with realizes they have a problem and feels a need to solve it if it's uncomfortable enough; they will be wide open to listening to you and your possible solution. They will be open to you because you will have acknowledged them and helped them clarify their issues. You will have won their trust because they're feeling good about you.

It's when you have asked enough questions, responded appropriately to their answers, discovered there is a need to make a change and hear, see or feel the signals that the other person is open to changing, that you propose that you might know of something that will help them.

PRINCIPLE #4: FEEDING BACK WHAT YOU THINK YOU HEARD THEY WANT

To ensure continual understanding, feeding back what you think you heard, or clarifying, is something you will soon learn to do on a constant basis throughout your conversation. The ultimate feedback is at the end of your conversation after you have gone through the process of discovery and you are presenting your solution. This is the time when you are in a position to summarize what the other person is looking for, why they are looking for it, and how you can help them get it. If you can feedback, recap and present this better than they can, you will have truly demonstrated a complete understanding.

I can remember a time when a lady called Barbara called to ask me about 'Natural Selling®.' She had read an article about Natural Selling® in a magazine and was exploring the idea that it might be something from which she could benefit. On being asked the question, "Could you tell me what Natural Selling® is all about?" I gave her a simple answer. *"You know how a lot of salespeople get anxious about selling because of all that rejection they have to go through? Well, Natural Selling® is a form of selling that is based on the desire to serve, doesn't use manipulation or techniques that cause rejection, and can get you the results you're looking for without the anxiety normally associated with selling. Would that be something you're looking for?"*

When she answered "Yes," I then kept the focus on her and started with a favorite question, *"Perhaps you could tell me more precisely what you're looking for?"* The conversation lasted about 10 minutes. During that time I said not one thing again about Natural Selling® or about me. I offered very few observations or statements when she answered my questions. I just asked questions around what she was doing and, in particular, around the challenges she faced. I listened, asked more questions, clarified and qualified as we progressed.

At the end of 10 minutes I asked her permission to allow me to feed back to her what I knew about her. During this time she twice stopped me and asked, "I said that?" I responded with, *"Is it true?"* and she replied, "Yes, but where did you get that from?" I then said, *"From you – where else would it have come from because we have never met before, have we?"*

Finally I asked, *"If Natural Selling® could help you solve these challenges and get you the results you're looking for by learning how to communicate more effectively, is that something you would like to happen?"* She answered, "Yes!"

I then asked her how *she* saw herself benefiting from taking a course with me! She gave me all the reasons based on how she saw her problems being solved by Natural Selling®. The interesting part is that I said very little about my program. All I said about it was in terms of relating what she was looking for as to how I could help her, and all of that was done at the end. The sale was cemented. Now it was a matter of talking about the fee. The fee was not an issue because the value was created within the conversation.

The point is, by not focusing on selling my services, but focusing on understanding her problems and getting behind them and getting them into perspective to see whether I could help, we both saw and understood her challenges more clearly, which reinforced her desire to be helped.

And you will do the same thing. When you understand what a person is really looking for, and why they want it, you will be able to customize your solution and present it in a way so that it personally means something to them.

SUMMARY

So these are the 4 principles of Natural Selling® – successful selling. It's all down to communication, coming from an inner place of calm and understanding of knowing what questions to ask, how to listen, what to listen for and eventually how to present your business opportunity.

The process of someone looking closely at your business opportunity, and buying it, is the result of you understanding how to make the 4 principles work. If there is a problem to be solved, you will discover it and offer a way to solve it. If there isn't, or if a person is not motivated to make a change, what will you do? You'll quickly move on to other opportunities.

Now, if there isn't a problem to be solved – have you lost a sale? No! Because there was never a sale to be made in the first place.

By understanding how to communicate in this way, do you think your anxiety about talking with people will disappear? Most probably it will – simply because you're not being rejected anymore. Because are you selling when you have these types of conversations? No, you're not. You're exploring and interviewing people to establish whether you can help them. It's not you selling them; it's now you qualifying them as to whether they have a problem and whether you can be of service. They, at the same time, are qualifying and selling themselves on the idea that it's time to change!

You Are The Solution!

You are, in fact, selling something though – yourself! You are a unique feature of your product or business opportunity. If a person buys you as a feature – do you think they will have a peek at the rest of what you're about? Of course. Sell the relationship first and the solution second.

And when you have these types of conversations, you will find that people will come to logical conclusions similar to the one that motivated you to get involved with your business. The logical conclusion is that many people will reveal they want to change from what they are doing. Your questions will allow them to surface their own deep inner desires that perhaps they had given up on long ago, and seriously look at getting their dream back in focus again.

And here is the real point: their motivation is different than yours. They will make changes for entirely different reasons, (internal reasons) than you. If you listen for, respect, understand and respond to their inner needs, you will not only discover what they are, you will also discover they will end up listening to you.

Next Step

In Part II we will look more closely at why these principles work and at the power of using Dialogue, the communication machine that will have people being drawn to you in a way you probably never could have imagined before.

43

Part II

Principle #1
Helping Other People
Solve Their Problems

Chapter 4:
The Power Of Dialogue!

Chapter 5:
Current Reality

Chapter 6:
The Discovery Process

CHAPTER 4

The Power Of Dialogue!

A feast of reason and the flow of soul.
– Alexander Pope

How Effective Are You At Communicating?

Do one or more of these things happen to you?

- Do you feel the discomfort of rejection when people respond negatively to you?

- In the process of talking with people, do you often feel frustrated because you can't get your point across and, consequently, you stop recruiting because of this frustration?

- When you have made a few sales, do you slow your efforts down, or start managing?

- When you discover someone interested in buying your products or business opportunity, are you afraid to ask for the order or for the commitment to take the next step, because you are uncomfortable with receiving the money as the reward for your efforts?

- When you make a sale, do you feel uncomfortable receiving the money from it?

Why is this? Well, much of it has to do with the communication model of telling and persuading that is used and taught in Network Marketing. The model tends to be self-focused and can be adversarial and doesn't connect with our soul. We inwardly question our actions and resist doing it.

Telling and persuading is out of step with the desire to help, serve and receive. Using the model of telling can subconsciously reinforce your negative feelings about money as well. From my own point of view, when I started selling and used techniques to get the sale, it didn't feel right to me. The result of that was that the money didn't feel honestly come by. Using techniques were reinforcing all the old sayings about money being the root of evil. (It's not. Greed is!) When I stopped the techniques and communicated with people differently, the money flowed faster and I received it with gratitude.

While this standard model of telling invariably contains the element of asking questions, most distributors don't ask enough of the right questions and, in my experience, don't listen for the right things and are all too anxious to get to the solution as quickly as possible. Asking someone what they would do if they could and then telling them, "If I could show you how to do that?" is not asking questions – it's too fast, too soon.

THREE MAIN COMMUNICATION MODES

Behavioral scientists have shown that in communicating with others, we are:

1. Least persuasive when we tell people things, or attempt to dominate them, (Presenting. Telling. Teaching. Persuading.)

2. More persuasive when we interact and discover from each other, (Discussion. Debate.)

3. Most persuasive when we allow others to persuade themselves, (Dialogue.)

While each of these ways of communicating has their use, the last one for us is the most important, if we want to be effective in selling and relationship building. It is however the least used because it is the least understood. Let's look at all three modalities:

PRESENTING, TELLING, TEACHING, PERSUADING

You learned in the previous chapters that the high incidence of rejection and objections regularly happens when using the classical approach of telling or presenting solutions or telling your story too early. In other words, the focus is on the need to tell your solution before first establishing if in fact the other person has a problem, the depth of it, and the circumstances around and behind it, and whether there is any real desire to make a change.

Presenting or telling people things can cause you personal tension, not to mention the tension it causes in the other person. *When I focus on me, I increase my anxiety.*

Presentations are usually prepared talks where the presenter attempts to grab and hold another person's attention early in the conversation, and move them toward taking an action step using external motivating techniques such as the fear of loss, greed, envy or guilt. These can be very powerful motivators, though the results are usually temporary.

The proof of the pudding is in the eating. Why do so many distributors or customers drop away? A major cause is that they get externally motivated, and when it comes time to take action, the motivation wears off. Reason? Real motivation comes from within!

WHY DISTRIBUTORS PRESENT

So why do people present if the results are questionable? Presenting is easy to do. Distributors like to present what they perceive to be the advantages of their business opportunities and products, because they only have to learn it once and then churn it out!

Presenting is safe. In fact, it's so safe that unless you're very good at it, few people respond!

Presenting is familiar territory. It makes the person who is doing the presenting feel in charge, in control. Ironically, the need to be in control can work against you. If you want to be in control, let go of the need. Letting go of the need allows you to be creative and open to possibilities. You allow you to be you. Your authenticity shows through and a relationship of openness, partnership and trust begins. Acting on the methods based on the principles in this book will allow you to make this work.

While presenting can work for some people – it doesn't for the majority, as presenting sounds canned – as if it's a 'one size fits all' solution. If you accept that we are all unique, then *does* one size fit all? The point is, if your meetings begin with a presentation, it begins with you talking about you, and what you think, and ends with you hoping that something in what you say will trigger off something that will get your potential associates to respond. But it's guesswork! Running through all the reasons with them as to why you're excited about what you've got or what you're doing, and why they should be as well, is very one-sided and untargeted.

You can't assume that because you're excited and enthusiastic, they are going to be as well. Their motivations for buying something, or making a change, is going to be different from yours, and from everyone else's. Also, if you approach someone with too much external enthusiasm, you stand either the chance of their withdrawing from you because you

> *Your enthusiasm can, in fact, be an asset that gets in your way.*

have overwhelmed them, or if they do get swept along in the current of your presence, what do they do when you've gone? They go back to their old habits because external enthusiasm is not part of their make-up. *Your enthusiasm can, in fact, be an asset that gets in your way.*

Think also what presenting is like for the person you're talking with? How do you think other people think and feel? That frozen smile on their face is just that – a frozen smile, behind which they are working out how to defend and protect themselves from you making them do something they don't want to do. While they are doing that, are they *listening* to you? Are they taking in anything you are saying? Hardly likely!

The two key things that people fear the most in being presented to, are:

1. Are you going to persuade them to do something they don't want to do or buy?

2. How much time are you going to take?

Presentations *are* important – properly done and in their right place – such as with a very large group where interaction is difficult, and when it's expected that you will present. The most fruitful time, as you're discovering, is at the end of a meeting when you have pulled all the facts together and your presentation is based on knowing precisely what the other person wants, why they want it, and being able to give it to them.

So, if traditional sales techniques of telling and presenting early in the conversation, serve neither you nor the person you're with, the question is, can other modes of communication serve you better?

DISCUSSION AND DEBATE

Discussion and debate is another way of communicating. The discussion mode is something with which we all are already familiar. We are used to expressing our own views with people, usually in the hope of winning them over to our side.

In his book, *The Fifth Discipline*, a book about learning, Peter Senge defines discussion as a conversation among two or more people where "Different views are presented and defended and there is a search for the best view to support decisions that must be made at this time." He goes on to suggest that this type of conversation is "Prone to fall into a game where the object of the game is to win by having your own ideas accepted by the other party. You might occasionally accept another's view to strengthen your own, but you want your view to prevail."

This type of approach in selling, where the object is to win your client over to your viewpoint, does not always fully explore, or allow you to give the same priority to the needs of the person with whom you are speaking, as your own. For example, if you handle someone's objections with "Yes, but . . . ." answers, you are attempting to persuade the other person to your point of view, even if you think the persuasion is for their benefit.

To give priority to the needs of the other person is difficult for many distributors and salespeople who have been taught to focus on the targeted outcome of the sale. Giving priority to the other person means letting go of control. And yet giving priority and exploring with others in a climate of trust is vital if you are to understand and help another person and yourself get what you both want. So, if you want to change the results, change the climate of communication.

Dialogue

Using Dialogue will bring about such a change of priorities. Dialogue is an open form of communication that will allow you to receive all the answers you need to find out the core essence of most people – what makes them tick, and whether you can help them. Your complete openness in communication tells the other person a lot about you and what you represent without you having to say very much. By having an open dialogue, you create a field of energy that makes people compelled to listen to you and your ideas. It's the dream of every distributor!

The Key Essence Of Dialogue!

In contrast to discussion, "We are not trying to win in a dialogue. We all win in a dialogue if we are doing it right." Peter Senge says. The purpose of dialogue is to go beyond each person's understanding so that, "collectively, we can be more insightful, more intelligent than we can possibly be individually."

Collective thought or truth, as we know, begins to make sense to the other person in the form of order and consistent harmony. "All of us," Senge says, "have had some taste of dialogue – in special conversations that begin to take a life of their own, taking us in directions we could never have imagined nor planned in advance. But these experiences come rarely, a product of circumstance rather than systematic effort and disciplined practice."

The key thing is that in using dialogue, you help people work out the inconsistencies of their own thoughts, come to their own conclusions, and be more open to the idea of change.

DIALOGUE AND NATURAL SELLING®

Dialogue is used on your Journey of Discovery with your potential partners. It achieves your purpose, (which is to serve) and, in doing so, helps you achieve your objectives. The three principles of asking questions, listening, and understanding through feedback are actually the *communication principles of dialogue*. They are the backbone of it.

This is the real meaning behind what Tom Peters said, "My job is not to sell products. My job is to solve problems!"

Dialogue is like playing chamber music where the sum total of all the different instruments, playing their individual scores, make up a resonance that enhances the sound of one instrument and, at the same time, is more harmonious than the sound of one instrument alone.

Dialogue requires you to detach from your expectations. For example, think about letting go of your attachment of making the sale and, instead, *focus on whether there is a sale to be made in the first place*. Feel the difference in energy from just realizing that. By detaching yourself from the outcome of making the sale, you become open to hearing, feeling and understanding the other person's priorities. It enables you to be creative and see expanded opportunities and ideas as to how their problems can be solved. It opens up the field of infinite possibilities. The end result can be even greater than what you expected!

In the process, you create new relationships or strengthen the ones you have regardless of the outcome. You can't help it. It happens! The focus is off you, on the other person, and both of you feel the magic of helping each other. Doing it is freeing. When I focus on me, I increase my anxiety. When I focus on you, I decrease my anxiety!

*When I focus on me,
I increase my anxiety.
When I focus on you,
I decrease my anxiety!*

THE MECHANICS OF DIALOGUE

Bohm, a communications researcher early in the last century, identified in his research three basic premises that are necessary for dialogue:

1. All participants must 'suspend their assumptions.'
2. All participants must regard one another as colleagues.
3. There must be a facilitator who 'holds the context' of dialogue.

What I've discovered is that you can achieve all of the above conditions in most conversations without having to explain the process of dialogue to the other person. Just doing it – just using the process itself automatically draws the other person into the spirit of things. We'll explore this!

1. Suspension Of Assumptions.

By suspending your own assumptions, judgments and prejudices and not allowing yourself to be drawn into arguing, debating or defending your point of view, and just simply listening without prejudice, you will find others will suspend their own defensive positions and be open to other beliefs and possibilities.

You don't have to agree with someone to listen to them. The return on investment in listening is huge. You learn a lot and people end up listening to you. It's the law of reciprocity.

In doing so, it's possible to come to a point where making a suggestion, such as, *"What if there was another way of looking at it, another way that would give you everything you wanted without any of the discomfort associated with your present way of doing things?"* . . . will cause most people to reflect on and shift their present beliefs. This is an example of allowing others to persuade themselves. Beliefs, after all, are just an acceptance of, or holding an opinion. People will challenge their beliefs if you appear to be open to challenging yours. Be prepared to challenge yours. You might find your own beliefs holding you back!

2. Becoming Colleagues

The sense of openness that dialogue has is an energy that is subconsciously picked up and conveyed right back to you. I've found that people will automatically become colleagues if you come from a place of not wanting to manipulate, but of wanting to understand before helping. People are drawn to people who are genuinely interested in them. Don't focus on your point of view of getting to your final objective of making the sale. Focus instead on the present moment and getting to understand the present situation or current reality of the person with whom you're talking.

3. You Are The Facilitator

Instead of having a facilitator, you become the facilitator. In dialogue you can take two roles – the observed and the observer. As the *observed* you are the one directly involved with the conversation at all its logical and emotional levels. As the *observer* you do two things. You facilitate the conversation for both you and the other person without prejudice, and you observe your own thinking, words and actions.

One of the great things about being the observer and the observed is that you can actively and emotionally participate in the dialogue and, at the same time, detach yourself from it and objectively observe and guide what is going on. This guidance is not designed for you to manipulate the outcome but to act as the 'honest broker,' to guide the conversation toward an outcome that is beneficial to all. By staying open and understanding more, it is incredible how bigger, more precise and stronger solutions will surface. One and one have a habit of not making two – they make eleven! *Effective dialogue is when real synergy occurs.*

CHANGING YOUR FUTURE RESULTS

By observing yourself, you also have additional benefits. For example, if a conversation 'falls off the tracks' or if it gets stuck, because of something you said or didn't know what to say, you can, in a quiet moment later, reflect on it and mentally change the result which will prepare you for the next time this might happen.

The key here is first of all not to beat yourself over the original conversation. It was what it was. Instead, replay the mental 'tape' of the conversation up to the point where it went astray. Edit out the actual end result from your mind. Get rid of it.

Now recreate what would have happened had you been more alert or more experienced by role-playing with yourself. Redefine it in your mind, and rehearse it. Feel the good feelings and park the satisfactory result somewhere in your subconscious. The subconscious mind doesn't know what you have done. It simply believes this new reality. What do you think will happen when the same or similar situation arises? You will move through it as though the barrier is nothing but a bead curtain. You have prepared for it. Your wisdom is that much greater.

Heed an Aikido saying: "Prepare for everything and expect nothing!" By mentally rehearsing and knowing how to deal with situations, you will always be prepared. So let it go and don't expect it to happen again. If it does – you will be prepared. Unfortunately, most distributors prepare for nothing and expect everything. This includes negative expectations such as objections. So, prepare for things like concerns and then don't expect them!

SOCRATES AND THE USE OF DIALOGUE

There have been many groups that used dialogue to make decisions or develop consensus in the past. Socrates (469-399 BC) – a stonemason and carver in Athens, at a time of great culture in Greece – is credited for refining the form of communication we know today as the Socratic Dialogue.

Socrates' purpose in life was to discover universal truth. He felt it his mission to test all statements, recommendations, explanations and personal truths! He questioned public and private men. He described himself as a midwife bringing other men's thoughts to birth and stimulating them to think and question their own beliefs, not through instruction, but by allowing them to listen to their own answers when he asked easy-to-answer questions.

The process he used was dialogue through conversation, which was revolutionary in his time. It suggested our destiny was not predetermined by the Gods but by the world of Cause and Effect. The process of dialogue allows us to arrive at a consensus – our own stories or truths that we can all agree on – change if we choose, and act on. The process is powerful and enlightening as it allows the person we are talking with to take back the responsibility for him/herself and take action to determine his/her future.

TEACHING AND THE USE OF DIALOGUE

The Socratic Dialogue is used in many universities to teach. At the renowned Duke University in Durham, North Carolina, where it forms the backbone of teaching, William Hall, Professor of Neurobiology explained to me that the tutor's role is one of a facilitator and participant, to guide students to have:

- A respect for varying points of view.
- A deeper and clearer consideration of the subject and ideas in question.
- Adherence to and respect to the process of dialogue.

Guiding the students through a process of intense listening, questions and feedback, and helping them stay open to all possibilities, the professor helps the students to learn to openly communicate and to think critically and solve problems with which they are faced.

Students at these universities demonstrate insights and psychological realizations that classical approach teachers overlook. Not only do students acquire information in a different way, they do so at the high end of the thinking/reasoning process.

Teachers, when they first use the Socratic Dialogue, sometimes have great difficulty in letting go of the need to be in control as the teacher. Being the one who knows and therefore has to teach, it initially can make them feel as though the dialogue might get out of control from not having predetermined questions with acknowledged answers.

It's the same challenge that distributors can have when changing from the 'classical selling' style where they feel they have to talk and present, to the Socratic style of Natural Selling®. However, as Ashley Montagu put it, "In teaching, it's the method and not the content that is the message – the drawing out, not the pumping in."

NATURAL SELLING® AND THE USE OF DIALOGUE!

By applying the method of communication Socrates used, and using principles of dialogue that are universal to all, you can have conversations that are comfortable and friendly for both of you. Conversations that will produce the results you, and the other person, are looking for without all the anxiety and stress that classical selling can bring you. Conversations with great endings!

Like the university professors, your role is an independent one. Observing the first principle of Natural Selling® – helping other people solve their problems – you start by removing yourself from the outcome of making the sale, and come instead from a place of intent to discover whether you can be of service. You ask simple easy-to-answer questions as an impartial observer, as well as the participant, and listen for ideas, (not what you think you're hoping to hear). Ask, listen, ask and stay open.

Using this process you subconsciously invite the other person to participate in the process merely by your actions (Cause and Effect). Later, both of you will come to a logical conclusion. What you come to can be greater than you ever expected.

As a distributor, the use of dialogue is a matter of helping people get to a point of lucid thought where, independent of all other influences, they make a decision to predetermine their own future. You help them find, re-discover or re-determine the inner freedom that many are seeking. It will liberate their soul – and allow them to see the real freedom they can choose to have, versus a life of safety and lack that comes from acquiescence and subjugation.

It is this point of clarity that is your *first* destination and objective in Natural Selling®. What I mean by this is that you will have explored through dialogue a person's history, their current reality, their feelings about where they are in the present, and what their future expectations are. You will both discover if there is need and the depth of their desire to change their present circumstances to meet the need. Dialogue brings another person's *Current Reality into the present moment.* This will be discussed in the next chapter. It's a process that will give both of you a clearer blueprint that will be self-evident as to what the next step will be!

Through dialogue, people consciously and subconsciously agree with themselves that they have the ability to make a change. Instead of you persuading them with all the classic techniques, they persuade themselves. They have the answers to what they want. It's just that they might not be using the right solutions. It's their decision to look at your solution should you choose to present it. And, if your solution looks good to them, they will end up owning the solution as opposed to being persuaded to take it on. They will give themselves the credit for finding it and you the credit for helping them. Perfect harmony!

If they decide to move forward, you offer your solution as a natural extension of your conversation for them to achieve what they are looking for. You customize your solution and give your solution personal meaning based on what you were told.

On the other hand, if they decide to stay where they are, that's fine. The time and circumstances might not be right for them. Respect that and bow out graciously. One thing is for certain. They will remember your conversation. Expect them to return at another time!

At this point the dialogue will have served its purpose and you can continue with a mixture of dialogue and discussion. Even so, you will find with experience, dialogue will still be a major part of how you communicate.

CHAPTER 5

Current Reality

Any one fool can come up with the answers. But the real measure of wisdom is coming up with the right questions.
– Swami Beyondananda

PAST – PRESENT OR FUTURE VISION?

If you tell someone early in a conversation you can help him or her make more money, make their health better, or make their life better, are you focusing on their Past, their Present Moment or their Future? It's their future!

And, if Current Reality can be defined as someone telling you the truth about where they are in their lives *right now*, whether they are (1) stuck in the Past somewhere, (2) living in the Present Moment, (3) or focused on the Future, where do you think most people are in their 'Current Reality'? In the Past, Present Moment or the Future? I think you'll agree it's their Past!

STUCK IN THE PAST

The Current Reality of most people is stuck somewhere in their Past – in their history. They got to a certain point in their lives where they accepted what they had as their lot in life. They then programmed themselves with personal defensive strategies to protect this position. They lowered their vision and found and mixed with others of the same thinking until their defensive strategy became so entrenched that their strategy became hidden even from themselves. That is the strength of it. It's hidden, and it gets fed constantly by external influences because they see the world as they are and not what it really is in all its glorious abundance. Subsequently, they continually settle for what they have and that is their Current Reality.

Their vision is one of getting by and phrases like these are giveaways to this kind of thinking and acceptance:

"I only need enough to get by!"

"One day my ship will come in . . . ?"

"You know, it's not like it used to be when . . . ."

"It will never happen to me."

"I've given up thinking about that . . . ."

And, therein, lies one of the problems of focusing on the future and telling people what you can do for them early in your conversation. There is no *context* or base on which to reflect what or where their Current Reality is at this very moment in time. There is no discussion or thought given to the circumstances that got them stuck where they are.

If you don't address or speak about their Current Reality and how they feel about it in the present moment, and your conversation is focused solely on the future, talking only about a person wanting more time to play golf, or to stay at home with the kids, for example, the chances are he/she will not persuade him/herself to change their present situation. There is also little chance for you to even make any sort of relationship or connection.

Also, only talking about the future is not a vision or dream for most people. It's a fantasy! That's why telling people what they should do, or telling your story at the beginning of a meeting, or asking them what they would do if they could do anything, and how your solution will get them what they want without anchoring it to what they don't have, and how they feel about it – rarely works.

A recent survey in North America showed that most of the population will not have enough to retire comfortably at age 65, and that 15% are relying on winning the lottery as their retirement income. That's over a 14 million to 1 chance – against! What that tells us is that many have given up on the idea of creating their own destiny by taking control of their lives. The reality is that many have conditioned themselves to accept where they are and live in a world where they have become prisoners of their own minds.

THE RESULT OF A LIFETIME OF NEGATIVITY

More and more people don't see the future holding any promise for them, because their social conditioning, everyday experiences and self-fulfilling thoughts and actions keep proving it. They have allowed all of the powerful influences of peers, families, institutions, etc., to creep in to take over their one responsibility in life – to themselves! They abrogate their responsibility to others in exchange for a piece of certainty, such as the government or institutions taking responsibility for issues they could settle themselves. They allow others to think and do things for them. And then they experience the ultimate truth – nothing changes. The only thing that does change is the loss of another bit of the freedom. The freedom they were seeking in the first place.

So they build walls of personal defensive strategies to protect themselves from their dreams because they have exchanged these dreams for the so-called security of the big machine of life – the regular paycheck, the medical benefits, the government handouts. The walls of their Current Reality become so thick that even if they could see what was their dream, they wouldn't know how to let it in. They become comfortable with being uncomfortable.

PERSONAL DEFENSIVE STRATEGIES HOLD THE PAST!

Why don't people live in the present moment? Because for most people, being in the present moment is too painful to think about. When they look at what they've got, or where they are, or where they are going, it doesn't look too good! Therefore, they make themselves content with what they've got. This, in itself, can be comfortable, as they don't have to face their shortcomings and bring up all the emotions associated with failed dreams, and non-perfect circumstances.

Would most people openly admit they live in the past and not in the present moment? Would they admit that they let life dictate what happens to them as opposed to them dictating the substance of their life? Not many will – directly! It can be too embarrassing to admit even to themselves that the veil of their apparent well-being is somewhat of a charade.

Few people will openly face their present situation because it may very well mean having to deal with a different reality – the present moment. What it really is!

Many have allowed their defensive strategies to be part of their thinking for such a long time that they don't even know it's happening any more. It's embedded. And that's its strength. Because it's embedded, because it is hidden from them it continually strengthens.

To face their Current Reality with all of its shortcomings is painful. It is much easier to do nothing, to cover the emotions with logic, excuses, rationalization, etc., as a way of not taking responsibility for their shortcomings or for what they don't have in life. It is much easier to blame others for being where they are. Facing reality in the present moment with its accompanying warts is painful. The pain represents what is missing internally and externally in their lives.

A promise of a better future is something people hear day after day and, if you do the same thing and thrust your solution at them too early, you'll be just another in a long line offering the fabled philosopher's stone. Unless you break the pattern – **your pattern** of behavior! If you do, most people will open up and tell you everything!

HELPING PEOPLE CHANGE

If you want to talk about someone's future – find out about the past first and bring it forward into the present moment. Then talk about the future bringing that into the present moment. *You heal the past and manifest the future – in the present.*

Look at your own thinking and action process. Why did you get involved with your own business? Almost certainly, because you came into the present moment and wanted to change what you had and where you were going. You saw your Current Reality as being stuck in the past and when you brought it into the present moment, you realized that this state of affairs was something with which you did not want to continue. You decided to change! You saw having your own business as the vehicle to make the change.

You can help others do the same as yourself. You can help them look at their Current Reality and evaluate if it is where they want to be. You can help them explore what it *means* and how it *feels* not having what they want. You explore what they have done to solve their problems, if anything, and how *that* felt! Then, finally you explore with them how it will *feel* when their problem is *solved.*

Our reality is nothing more than our own translation of what is happening in the world based on our own experiences. Those who feel uncomfortable with and want to escape from the social hypnosis of social conditioning and personal experiences of being a victim, are the ones who can start to move forward in their lives and get the experiences they are looking for. It's all energy and it starts from within. It's a new belief taken from ancient wisdoms of, "Wherever I am, I am the master."

THE PROCESS. THE OBJECTIVE. YOUR PATH.

When you help a person through this process of discovery by using dialogue, you allow people to see themselves where they are more clearly. Thus it empowers them in the sense that they are now in a position to see their situation as it is in the present and decide whether they wish to return to where they are, or to change and take action to move forward if it is too uncomfortable to bear. If it's uncomfortable, it reinforces why they are where they are, and that changing will have more significance to them.

Unless people are willing to see themselves in the present situation, they will continue to act as a continuation of their past. If they acknowledge their situation in the present and feel the full brunt of their discomfort, then they will seriously look at taking action to achieve their vision.

USING DIALOGUE

By listening and asking questions through dialogue, you can help another person examine his/her prior decisions and beliefs, and by feedback and clarification come to an understanding of how they arrived at the position they are in now. Chances are where they are now is not where they want to be.

TENSION

Facing this reality might create tension and may be uncomfortable. At this point a person will either face up to their situation and make a decision to creatively make a correction, or they will withdraw to avoid the pain of being in the present moment. *Some people prefer what they know and are familiar with, rather than deal with the Present Moment.*

TENSION SEEKS RESOLUTION. MOVING FORWARD OR STAYING BACK.

The resolution of tension can either be Creative – moving forward to resolve and get rid of it with different solutions, or Non-Creative – returning to the status quo. Results will be achieved either way. They will either get the ones they would really like by traveling different roads and resolving this tension by making a decision to achieve their goals, or they will continue along the ones they have allowed life to deal them!

NON-CREATIVE TENSION

If negative emotions surface and the feelings from seeing themselves in the present moment is uncomfortable for them, and they get defensive, remember, it's not about you. It's a reflection of their own discomfort with themselves and you get to see it and see what is their reality with it.

Be comfortable with their discomfort, and not take it on or let it affect you. It's not your baggage. You're there to help and if you take on their baggage now there are two of you carrying it. So allow yourself to be free of this so that you can observe impartially if they are willing to change, and whether you can help them by becoming a potential business partner. Being comfortable with it also means you are accepting it for what it is and you can stay creative.

Some will find it too uncomfortable to even talk about it. You'll ask a question and you might get a confused answer or no answer at all. The reason is that when people hear their own words, they have to face their own reality – now! It's doubtful that a person who is in this state is someone you can help. After all, can you really help people? No, only they can help themselves. You can only assist them in doing so, if they are willing. So the question is, if a person you're talking with cannot accept his or her own personal reality and cannot face making a change, is this someone you want to have on your team? It's your team. You decide!

Depending on the depth of the conversation, one thing is for sure, whether they join you or not, they will remember the conversation. If you don't pressure them and allow them some space, it's likely they will come back and continue the conversation with you at a later time after they have filtered the conversation. It's like planting seeds. Seeds have a tendency to germinate at different times. Your business can grow with the seeds you have planted in previous times if you come from a place of giving and detachment.

If they are not prepared to make a decision, and prefer to stay where they are, then you are in a position to thank them for their time and look for someone else who will be a stronger asset to your organization. Keep on sowing the seeds and nurturing them.

CREATIVE TENSION

However, if they are prepared to make a change, and have not been pressured or put under duress, coercion, or manipulation on your part, then they will consider your business opportunity with an open mind. Whether they buy your solution or not depends on whether you can customize what you have to offer, to answer what they need. If the business opportunity fits their needs and desires, you will have a motivated business partner.

Creative tension arises from the difference between Current Reality and the future vision. Unlike Un-Creative tension, which is based on negative emotions, Creative tension gives rise to excitement, the infinite possibilities that arise from changing the status quo.

THE PRESENT MOMENT IS THE KEY TO THE FUTURE

Nevertheless, regardless of the outcome, because of the process of having touched their soul, you will develop powerful allies to help you in your quest – a circle of influence, which will bloom from that one point of contact.

This is the magic of Natural Selling®; it is a win/win situation for all. Nobody loses – everybody gains. You only do business with people who naturally need what you have to offer. You have a place. And, above all, your success breeds a strong sense of understanding and community. By using the process of dialogue you have demonstrated a way to communicate that empowers people to make decisions.

So now it's time to build on the principles you have learned, now that we have rediscovered what selling really means! It's now time to take action – to make this actually work for you and the people you talk with, increase your success rate, have happy relationships with people you don't know, and strengthen the relationships with people you do know – regardless of whether they buy anything from you!

Your next step is to put a structure on top of these principles and learn how to do this, using your own style and personality.

CHAPTER 6

The Discovery Process

Most people don't see the world as it is.
They see the world as they are.
– Anna And The King

THE DISCOVERY PROCESS

The core concept of Natural Selling® is The Discovery Process, where your objective is to have a conversation with someone, and come to a destination point or a Logical Conclusion as to whether:

- He/she does not have a problem with their Present Situation.

- He/she does have a problem with their Present Situation and has no desire to change it.

- He/she does have a problem with their Present Situation, and is prepared to resolve it.

How do you do you find this out? By:

- Asking questions.

- Listening.

- Responding to the answers with more questions to find out more.

What do you talk about? You discuss three areas of their life:

1. Their Current Reality (past history).

2. The Present Moment.

3. Their Future Desires.

All of the above categories interact with each other to become a harmonious whole. When you've found there is a problem and an interest in solving it, you offer your solution as a natural extension of your conversation to explore whether your solution will work for them.

A Mutual Journey Of Discovery

On the next page there is a Conversational Framework called The Discovery Process that will allow you to do this. You can look on this framework as being the Communication Framework of dialogue that makes the 4 Principles work for you.

The Framework is like having instructions that will allow you to plot a *'Mutual Journey of Discovery'* with any person you're talking with. The intent is to find out about each other. You will, by the nature of putting all the focus on the other person, find out a lot more about them than they will about you. However, what will they find out and discover about you is that you care, appreciate and understand them. They will automatically trust and like you. A rare commodity!

It's all in the process. The outcome of each conversation is not a result of how well you use closing or objection handling techniques; it's how well you can understand and respond to the other person *during* the journey.

The sales dialogue you will learn does not take the approach of ending up as one big 'yes' or 'no'. It is a series of internal decisions made by your potential partner as he/she progressively concludes that you *understand* what they really want and that you can be trusted to work in their interest.

The outcome of the other person listening to your solution and buying from you is a result of the integrity of the process. It's also the result of how well you listen to, understand and can talk about a person's challenges before talking about how your business opportunity can alter that.

The Framework

The Conversation Framework is a guideline... a directional guide to help you draw a road map of a person's life and history, from where they have come (Their Past), where they are in their life (Their Current Reality), how they see themselves

Natural Selling® Conversation Framework
The Discovery Process

1 Connecting Stage

CONNECTING QUESTIONS
Demonstrates your intent. Puts focus on other person.

2 Discovering Stage

BACKGROUND QUESTIONS
Finds the present situation - the basic facts.

NEEDS AWARENESS/ DEVELOPMENT QUESTIONS
Explores needs/problems if any. *What* your customer wants.
Explore circumstances causing the needs. *Why* your customer wants it.
Reveals the correct features, advantages and benefits to solving the problem.

CONSEQUENCE QUESTIONS
Expands on the problems.
Makes the need more urgent.
Explores consequences of making a wrong decision.

SOLUTION QUESTIONS
Involves your customer and their ideas.
Reveals and strengthens the benefits of solving the problem.

QUALIFYING QUESTIONS
Confirms if other person is ready to take action.

3 Transitioning Stage

TRANSITION QUESTIONS
Opens the door to presenting your solution.

4 Presenting Stage

SUMMARY AND AGREEMENT
Confirms the correct solution. Presents the specific features, advantages
& benefits of the solution that solves the problem and satisfies the needs.

5 Committing Stage

COMMITMENT QUESTIONS
Helps other person to commit or take the next steps.

L I S T E N

For a free LARGER copy of this chart, go to
www.NaturalSelling.com/charts.html

at this moment in time (Their Present Situation), and where they would like to go (Their Future – dreams and desires). It will help you unravel and understand the unique mystery of each person with whom you talk.

With it you can have an open dialogue where every conversation is unique unto itself, to help you and your potential partner think through their present circumstances and how they arrived to this point in time.

The Conversation Framework gives you the five stages of a conversation, with the structure and different types of questions to ask in each stage. Understanding when, how, what and why you ask certain questions at certain times will help you constantly evaluate and understand the important elements of what people want.

In later chapters I will explain in more detail what those questions are and why you're asking them. At this point you will get an overview of the foundation – the big picture and the 'why' you're doing this before getting down to the details.

ANCHOR THE DISCOVERY FRAMEWORK IN YOUR MIND

Learn and imprint the structure of this framework and project it to the front of your mind when talking with people, just as you would see the image from an overhead projector being cast up on to a screen. Make it part of your conscious and subconscious. It will act as a valuable guide for you to know where you are at any particular time in your conversation.

While it is conceivable to linearly follow the different stages of the guideline as outlined on the framework, conversations usually don't co-operate that way. They tend to free flow. That is what makes them interesting and you'll discover you can move quite freely within the framework. In fact, you will! As new information comes to light, you will find yourself returning to the different stages, especially Stage 2 – The Discovering Stage. Use the different stages and question types with flexibility.

A CONVERSATIONAL ROAD MAP

Without a Conversation Framework like this, it would be like driving from Los Angeles to Chicago and having a map with no cities or roads on it! You would have no idea where to start or how to get there!

THE ANSWERS TO YOUR QUESTIONS CREATE THE MAP!

The Conversation Framework allows you to draw the other person's map with Chicago being any one of the three logical conclusions you are seeking. The way you get to see the starting point and roads to get to Chicago is to ask questions. The answers you get to your questions are like signs on signposts to steer you in the direction you want to go.

One signpost could yield more than one sign. You simply choose the sign (answer) that appears to have the most importance with regard to the direction you're going, and ask another question related to it that takes you to another signpost with more signs on it.

You start by going back in time and asking questions about their past and listening to them talk about their history. You ask about the circumstances that brought to them to this point in time – the present. You ask more questions to have them expand on what they said. In this way, you get to see the route and paths they took to get to the present moment. You then continue the journey and ask questions and talk about future possibilities and dreams. Doing this helps people get a picture of where they have come from, where they are now and where they would like to go. You move progressively toward one of the three logical conclusions.

For example, if you discover they are uncomfortable with their present situation, you can test to see whether their discomfort is strong enough for them to make a meaningful change by asking a Qualifying Question. If they indicate they want to make a change, you present your customized solution. You then continue your Journey of Discovery that are the next stages on the framework to complete your destination, which is the sale or next action steps.

Remember to listen to the answers. Your questions will come from the answers to your previous questions! And don't assume everyone knows their past, present and future visions! Many have buried their dreams and desires along with the debris of their so-called failures. Your questions bring their dreams to the surface.

The framework then gives you the ability to see how to map out their history and the circumstances that got them to this point in time. Getting to the logical conclusion or first destination is your own individual journey with the person with whom you're talking. You and I would do it differently. We might take different routes, but we would both get there. Depending on our skill and experience in asking questions and listening, one of us might get there a little faster or with more depth of understanding. However, it's not a race, it's a matter of understanding.

The beauty of this is that by asking questions and listening, a powerful bond is created between the two of you as you form a historical reference point of understanding on which you can build. Both of you get to see this and the map as it unfolds because you're both involved in it. It's definable and measurable with the immediate results of clarity, positive feedback, and no rejection if you listen and don't get eager to jump in with your solution too soon.

THE LOGICAL CONCLUSIONS

Logical Conclusion #1

One logical conclusion could be that they are content with their present situation. In this case your business opportunity probably will not have much impact on them and they probably won't be motivated to make a change or adjustment. I'm not saying they won't join you. All I'm saying is that the chances are they won't. It's just a logical conclusion. If that's the case, you might want to consider moving on to other opportunities where you can help.

You also might want to consider feeling joy and gratitude for this person in that they have what they want. Demonstrating feelings like that show you are coming from a place of abundance. Feelings and expressions of abundance are rewarded by abundance. It's a natural law of Cause and Effect!

In their interesting book called *Wisdom at Work*, Joel & Michelle Levey say, "Both ancient teachings and modern medical research agree that one of the quickest, most direct routes to restoring harmony and balance in our lives is to foster gratitude and appreciation. The moment you shift from a mind state of negativity or judgment to one of appreciation, there are immediate effects at many levels of your being: brain function becomes more balanced, harmonized, and supple; your heart begins to pump in a much more coherent and harmoniously balanced rhythm; and biochemical changes trigger a host of healthful balancing reactions throughout your body."

"In the wisdom ways of indigenous people, the restorative power of gratitude was well understood. A heart filled with gratitude generates actions and prayers that complete the circle between the gift offered to us, the receiver of the gift, and the sacred source of the gift."

On the other hand, a feeling of disappointment because perhaps it doesn't look as if a sale is going to be made, shows lack and will be rewarded by lack. If you feel lack, change the energy to abundance by feeling gratitude. Feel good for them and that they are happy with what they have and where they are. By exchanging the energy in you, you automatically change what happens to you!

Logical Conclusion #2

A second logical conclusion is that you discover a person *is* unhappy with their present circumstances and not really prepared to do anything about it. Perhaps they don't like their work, can't find work, can't make enough money, or any number of other reasons that is causing their unhappiness. Perhaps they might have even indicated initially they would change if they could. However, there is a difference between wanting to make a change and *doing* something about it. This is important to understand. Some people will say they are unhappy and would like to do something else, but when it comes to making the change to do it, they won't for a lot of reasons that are personal to them. Without a strong desire there is no lasting action, and without action there will be no change – for them or for you!

If you establish a person does have a problem but has no desire to do anything about it, you have to ask yourself whether you want to spend any further time talking about it, or even introducing how you might help. The choice is yours, though I would suggest at this point you again think of gracefully bowing out and look for other opportunities. A person will only change when they want to change. If you motivate them to do so externally, there is a great chance they will stop later, as you have already learnt in the previous chapter, 'Current Reality' and possibly through your own experiences.

Logical Conclusion #3

The third logical conclusion – and this is where you can start being of help – is when another person states they are unhappy with their present situation and have told you, directly or indirectly, they would like to do something about it.

NEXT STEPS

These 'conclusions' occur during The Discovering Stage of the Process, when you qualify a person by literally asking them if they would change if they could. If they state that 'yes' they are seriously looking to change, you can proceed to the Third Stage of the framework, which Transitions you into the Fourth Stage where you Present your customized solution.

After that, you continue your journey to your next destination, which is the Fifth Stage, the Commitment Stage, which could be the sale itself, or an agreement to take some action steps before the concluding agreement.

That's it in a nutshell!

LISTENING

While the Framework concentrates on the questions to ask, an equally powerful element is listening. Listening is the other key to discovering. Listening allows you to work out what questions to ask next to skillfully use the right questions at the right time to find out more and to bring your conversations to a logical conclusion. Listening guides you to one of your destinations!

LISTENING TO DISCOVER

Knowing how to listen and what to listen for are the two most valuable life skills you can learn from the point of view of being a successful distributor and being successful in your life in general.

It's only when you know how to listen, and what to listen for, can you hear, feel, and see the Current Reality of others and understand their real needs.

There are always reasons why people want what they want, and do what they do. They are usually personal psychological reasons. If you ask and listen, your potential partners will tell you! They have all the answers to what they want, but don't usually have the right solution. And you might! All you need do is listen and find out!

If you're familiar with personal growth programs, you'll know there is a great emphasis on discovering first of all what is causing or preventing you from getting what you want, then writing down what you want, why you want it and then thinking only of how to get it. Similarly this approach to changing your life and setting goals is what you are helping other people do with your questions. As I've mentioned before, *the answers to your questions are just as much for the other person as they are for you.* And your job is to discover those people who want to change, because helping others solve problems is where the opportunity is. It's where the money is! A problem solved can bring you and the recipient good fortune.

YOUR OBJECTIVE MUST BE MET AS WELL

While the first principle of Natural Selling® is about helping others get what they want, you must also get what you want. It's important not to lose sight of the fact that you do have an objective. If you don't realize your objective, you will be out of balance. You can't keep giving without receiving something! You'll end up broke and embittered. Learn to be open to receiving. Giving and receiving is, in essence, the same thing.

So while you do have an agenda, I like to call it a Conditional Agenda. Let your Conditional Agenda guide and not manipulate your questioning.

The purpose of the next two chapters is to enable you to actually hear, feel and see the reasons why people do what they do, think the way they think, feel the way they feel, say what they do, and why they will change.

First, please take the Listening Test on the next page before proceeding to the next chapter on How To Listen.

Test Your Listening Habits

Here is a short test that will give you an idea of your own listening habits:

When you're listening to someone,

- Do you think about other things while you're keeping track of the conversation?   Y   N

- Do you think about what you're going to say next?   Y   N

- Do you listen with the intent to reply rather than with the intent to understand?   Y   N

- Do you break in with your own ideas before the other person has finished talking?   Y   N

- Do you listen primarily for facts rather than ideas?   Y   N

- Do you 'tune out' to things that you feel will be too difficult to understand?   Y   N

- Do you try to make it appear you're paying attention when you're not?   Y   N

- Do certain words or phrases prejudice you so that you don't listen objectively?   Y   N

- Do your thoughts turn to other things when you believe a speaker will have nothing particularly interesting to say?   Y   N

- Do you finish other people's sentences?   Y   N

- Can you tell from a person's appearance and delivery that he/she won't have anything important to say?   Y   N

- Are you easily distracted by outside sights and sounds?   Y   N

If you answered 'NO' to all of these questions, you are one of a kind! From an early age, most of us are taught to express ourselves to get our points across. Very few of us are taught how to listen. Good listening habits can be learned.

Part III

Principle #2
Listening To What Is Being Meant,
Not Just What Is Being Said

Chapter 7:
How To Listen Effectively

Chapter 8:
Knowing What To Listen For

Chapter 9:
Presenting Your Solution – Satisfying Needs

CHAPTER 7

How To Listen Effectively

Success comes to those who listen

The act of open listening, listening without judgment, prejudice or interpretation, putting your agenda to one side and focusing on the other person, is so powerful that, if approached with good intent, will attract people to you like a magnet!

Put on top of that the ability to ask questions, knowing how to listen and what to listen for, (listening for the meaning) so you can ask further questions to gain deeper understanding, will create a field of energy that will further draw people to you. It will automatically differentiate you from most others. This is listening with your heart as well as your mind. If you doubt this, then I draw you again to a wonderful book called HeartMath that proves this and takes it beyond clichés and words!

Prove this for yourself **right now**. Drop this book and call or go out and find someone to speak with. Start a conversation and do nothing more than listen to the answers and ask questions based on the answers they give you. That's all! Don't make any statements, don't agree with anything, don't sympathize, don't offer any suggestions, don't talk about your own experiences, don't interrupt, just merely listen and ask interesting questions from the answers you get to your questions. Observe the other person. You'll notice they will relax, probably tell you a lot of personal information, get very chatty and, at the end of it, thank you for your time.

Effective Listening

Being heard and understood is a rare commodity and virtually non-existent in the world of selling and anywhere else! Effective listening takes work. The rewards, however, are outstanding, because listening forces you to slow down before trotting out quick questions. Slowing down means your questions will have a better quality. Better quality questions will reveal better quality answers!

It's all wonderfully synergistic, because asking questions and listening go hand in hand. Without one, the other is poorer for it.

Lazy listening dilutes the power of communication and especially your questions because you are likely to ask further questions based on the wrong elements of the answer. Many conversations are like this. The next time you're out, listen unobtrusively to others' conversations and you'll discover that there are usually two conversations going on and each person barely notices it!

LISTENING CREATES VALUE IN YOU AND WHAT YOU REPRESENT!

Asking questions and listening is a gift that you give. It shows you care and respect who they are, what they are and what they are saying. Paying attention to someone is one of the greatest gifts you can give, and what you receive is immeasurable.

Make sure you give this gift with good intent and with love. In return, you will find most people will want to listen to you, be associated with you and perhaps do business with you! The value of you and what you represent soars!

There is an interesting story about listening and value. Two ladies were talking about their hairdresser. One was commenting on how expensive he was and the other replied, "Yes! But he listens divinely!" That is what I mean by value!

LISTENING MAKES YOU SMARTER

Listening makes you appear smart. You also become smarter. It's a fact that the most successful and happy salespeople are good listeners. They know the only way they can help a person change is to understand them first. You can't do that by talking. Actually you can, but it's so hit or miss, so why do it?

They also know, like Tom Peters, that their job is not to sell products or services – their job is to solve problems. The more you listen, the more you put your agenda aside, the more you hear and the more creative you become. This opens up what Deepak Chopra calls the field of 'infinite possibilities!' The end result is usually far greater than you can imagine.

LISTENING ELIMINATES MISTAKES

We've all been in situations where we thought we had listened to someone's instructions only to find later that what they meant was not what we heard, and the job was not completed to their satisfaction. Most of us end up blaming the other person for their inadequate communication. This can be costly in terms of time and relationships.

The truth is, being disciplined and taking 100% of the responsibility for communicating eliminates costly mistakes and, at the same time, is a freeing experience. Next time you are given an instruction, take time out and repeat the instruction back with the words, *"Let me see if I've got this right! You said, " . . . (and repeat what they said and end with), "is that the way you see it?"* When giving an instruction, you can use the words: *"Just so that I know I conveyed those instructions correctly, would you feedback to me what is to be done?"* That is taking 100% responsibility. It also has a magnetic effect. If your business requires you to give instructions, you'll find that people will pay more attention to you, knowing that you're going to ask them to give feedback for clarification. They will also start copying your good habits!

FOUR RULES OF EFFECTIVE LISTENING

Listening is not an intellectual pursuit. Nothing changes unless you do, so if the Listening Test you took revealed that your skills in listening could be improved, then take steps to improve them! Below you will find four ways to do so. I suggest you read them, think about them, do them and then BE them.

The four rules can best be illustrated and understood by putting yourself on the receiving end and reflecting on how you feel when people do not listen to you. From the following illustrations, you can decide whether or not you behave the same way as others behave to you. If you do, you can decide whether your behavior is serving you and, if it's not, you can choose to change it.

Rule #1: Be Present

Have you ever had a conversation with someone in a restaurant, and a waiter or waitress walked by and the person you're talking with looked away from you to look at him or her? Or, have you ever been in the middle of a story and someone started up another conversation with someone else? Or, have you spoken to someone about an experience you had and the other person broke in and said, "I've had an experience like that – let me tell you what happened to me?"

What was that like? How did you feel? What was running through your mind at that time? Were these some of the feelings you had:

Annoyed?	Invalidated?
Unimportant?	Discounted?
Disrespected?	Frustrated?
Unheard?	Discredited?

What did the other person seem to communicate to you by their actions? That they were not being present and attending? How would you have liked the other person to behave? You probably would have liked him/her to have listened to you and not have thought about or observed other things. It's about being in the present moment. So if you're doing any of this, break the pattern of your behavior.

Being 'In the Present Moment' means:

- Concentrating on the speaker. Giving him/her your undivided attention, listening to everything they have to say. Making them feel they are the only person there.

- Using your body language, such as giving good eye contact, which demonstrates you're interested and paying attention. Or, if on the phone, make sure you are not doing other things.

- Not thinking about what you're going to say or ask next and, thereby, giving the other person your full attention.

This alone will make you different from most other people.

Remember that one of the reasons you don't have to worry about what to ask next is that while you will memorize some of your questions, most of your questions will come from the answers you get to your previous questions. You must keep your mind clear to listen to the answers.

RULE #2: BE ACKNOWLEDGING

Have you ever spoken with someone who sat motionless in front of you, hardly moved a muscle, and never spoke? If that's happened to you, how did you feel?

Frustrated?

Ignored?

Asking yourself, "What's wrong with me?"

How would you have liked them to respond? Perhaps move a little or acknowledge what you're saying? Acknowledging someone can have profound effects on your ability to draw others to you. So what are the keys to this?

The mechanics of acknowledging include:

Body Language

Same as in being in the present moment, these are nonverbal actions such as having good eye contact and leaning forward, nodding your head.

Feeding Back, Summarizing And Clarifying

A major cause of communication failure is interpreting what someone is saying based on your own experiences, beliefs, understandings and ego. Have you ever found yourself sympathizing with someone over something they told you, only to have egg on your face because you misunderstood where the other person was coming from?

Remember the story of the lady in chapter 2 who was talking with a friend of hers, about her husband leaving her and her friend was sympathetically saying how awful it must have been for her and she replied she was, in fact, happy to have him out of her life? This happens all the time in communication, and whether you like it or not, this type of behavior raises tension levels. It is another demonstration of jumping in with conclusions – conclusions based on having a different interpretation of what the other person is saying.

If you want to have full understanding and empathy with another person, ask questions before making your comments. Instead of saying for example, "You must be feeling awful" (unless you really know how someone feels!) find out and get feedback on a regular basis. Ask for their point of view to make sure you're both on the same track. Use phrases like:

> *"So, how do you feel about that?"*
> *"Let me see if I've got this . . . ."*
> *"So, what you're saying is . . . ?"*
> *"If I'm hearing you correctly . . . ."*
> *"I sense that you're upset about that . . . , is that right?"*

Verbal Pauses

These are 'sounds' that come out of your mouth to let the other person know you're there. Such as:

> *"Is that right?"*
> *"Oh, I see."*

"Wow!"

"Tell me more."

"Hmm!"

They let your potential partner know you are with them. Openly laugh at people's jokes if you think they are funny. I used to be a silent laugher. Not much noise came out of my mouth but I would be rollicking around inside. I didn't know this until I told a joke to three other silent laughers. I now laugh out loud!

Silence And Pausing!

The use of silence and allowing another person to think about your questions without breaking in is one of the most rewarding things you can do. Be 'still.' You will hear more about another person than you ever thought possible. Many times you will be told things they would never tell anyone else. If you doubt me, take into account a popular TV program called *Taxicab Confessions*, where drivers of taxis, who have hidden cameras and microphones in cabs, draw out the amazing real life stories of riders they pick up. If you are a good interviewer and you shut up long enough, like the drivers, it's incredible what you will hear people say!

The Discomfort Of Silence

Do you find yourself doing one or more of these three things immediately after you've asked a question and a person goes silent on you?

> Answer the question for them!
>
> Ask more questions!
>
> Change the subject!

Why is this? Why is it we are uncomfortable with silence? Why is it when there is a gap in the conversation there is an urge to fill in the 'gaps' or 'space'? Doing so breaks the tenet: *Silence is never more golden than when you hold it long enough to get all the facts and feelings before you speak.*

I have seen more sales conversations ruined by a distributor who has asked a pertinent question, only to answer it him/herself with an example or two, and take the conversation in another direction. Doing this leaves the other person feeling bewildered and invalidated. Why ask any question if you're not going to let people answer it in their own words?

The reason we don't like silence is because of our fear of losing control of the conversation. The opposite is actually true. Being quiet puts you more in control. Letting go of the control will allow you to have more of what you want. As Senator Dominick Barbara so eloquently put it, "You ain't learning nothin' while you're talking!" Stop talking and it will allow the other person to let you see what they are all about.

The Answer Might Not Be The One You Want

It also doesn't matter what their answer is. It is what it is. If you're still attempting to get the answers you want, that's all they will be, your answers! Not theirs! Manipulating answers can make people temporarily motivated, and, as you have discovered, that motivation does not last very long and they either stop taking your products or don't continue with the business.

They Might Ask You A Question That You Don't Want To Hear

If you're thinking it, they probably will, so stop thinking about it! Prepare for the most common questions, answer them and learn how to put a question at the end of your reply. For example:

> "Is this Network Marketing?"
>
> *"Yes, it is! Do you know anything about it?"*

You don't know why they asked, so acknowledge the question and ask why. Asking for clarification will reveal why the question was asked. I've had people reply, "Yes! I've heard you can make a lot of money at that."

Use The Power Of Silence

When you ask a question – *be quiet* and be comfortable with the silence. Being quiet is not a technique or a 'closing' trick. This is simply common courtesy. It allows the person you're talking with to reflect on and surface his or her own answers. My experience has demonstrated that the first answers you get are the first layer of the onion and the more you peel, the more different the answers become. There are a lot of truths and somewhere in the essence of the person is their real truth. It's just a matter of helping them find it!

So, give time for a person to think, even if it's for a minute or more. Don't break in to answer your own questions, make suggestions or change the subject. The mind is like a computer, sometimes it needs to search through the hard drive and sort itself out before coming up with an answer. When it does it's quite usual to receive more and deeper information than you had thought possible. Listening patiently can have infinite rewards! *Remember the maxim: 'Silence is …GOLDEN.' For both of you!*

RULE #3: BE ACCEPTING

A favorite piece of wisdom comes from an old Sufi saint saying, "Beyond the wrong doing, and beyond the right doing, there is a field. I'll meet you there!" This premise forms the foundation for what I believe is the most powerful aspect of listening and most other things in life.

Have you ever had the experience of someone telling you something that you felt in your mind was wrong, and against your own inner core values? Perhaps it was something you knew from your own experience was unacceptable, and you started arguing or debating with that person?

Or did you ever handle someone's objections with your, "Yes, but . . . .' answers that put your point of view over theirs?

Did you ever win the discussion? Did you come away from it full of joy because you managed to 'tell them?' Did you ever feel the other person changed their point of view? Probably not!

What do you think might have happened if, despite your desire to make your own point, you had listened to the other person? What if, in fact, you went further than this? You even asked them to expand on where they were coming from by asking principled questions to get to the reasons why they thought this way? And what if you did all of this, without judgment, assumptions or personal interpretation.

What would have happened is that:

- You would have gained more understanding.
- The other person might have subconsciously questioned and/or evaluated their thinking and beliefs as they listened to themselves answering your enquiring questions.
- It might have made the person reconsider their position and even change.
- They would have been more inclined to listen to you and your point of view.

It's reciprocity. It's a result of the respect you showed to their point of view, without you having to condone their thinking or compromising your own core values.

LISTENING AND ACCEPTING

IS A VERY POWERFUL PERSONAL PERSUADER

Listening and accepting without judgment doesn't mean you have to alter your mind. *You don't have to agree with someone to listen to them!* And suspending your assumptions about how you see the world and freeing yourself to see another person's has its own special rewards. The main ones being that you present yourself as an accepting, knowledgeable and interesting person, and someone worth listening *to!*

Their subjective reality is unique to them just as yours is to you. And everyone is right! Sometimes you need to listen to others with whom you don't agree. Accept others as they are. People see things in a different way than you. For example, if I'm holding a coin between my fingers and at arm's length in front of me so you are seeing the head of the coin, and I ask, *"What do you see?"* You would say you see a coin. I would say that I'm seeing a coin as well. While we both see the coin, we're seeing it from different perspectives. You are looking at the head and I'm looking at the tail. Imagine if both of us were unaware there was a head and a tail. The chances are that our conversation about the coin would be all over the place. It would be like digging a tunnel from opposite sides of a mountain, without knowing where the other team was, hoping we would meet in the middle. We would probably end up with two tunnels! It can be the same with conversations.

If you start by accepting where the other person is, and then explore more deeply into what the other person is seeing, and perhaps even feeling, you get to understand their perspective. And, as you do, and as you continue to accept their perspective, the energy field of openness, resulting from you letting go of the need to be right, is contagious. Others open up themselves.

For me this is the very essence of dialogue – the suspension of my own beliefs and prejudices so that I can understand the other person. By detaching myself from having to tell, from being drawn into debate, from stating or defending my point of view, I create an energy of calmness. From that the creative mind

When you stop insisting, people stop resisting.

goes into high gear where ideas in the form of questions flow quite easily. *When you stop insisting, people stop resisting.*

If you want others to change, change yourself first. You can listen people into changing by staying open with a desire to understand. You will also hear things you have never heard before. Things that were always there except you never listened and asked about. The result of this will give you a greater understanding of people, and they will have a greater understanding and respect for you. Listen and accept others and others will listen and accept you!

The keys to being accepting are to:

Accept Without Judgment

Don't judge others by your own subjective reality. Deepak Chopra puts it this way, "Being judgmental is only a reflection of your own moral righteousness." Also, your judgment of someone does not change him or her. It merely demonstrates your need to judge. By not making judgments, you set yourself free. The first step to becoming 'judgment-free' is to simply be aware of your judgments and decide to progressively eliminate this behavior.

Do this as an exercise. Next time when you're driving, and someone cuts you off on the highway, instead of getting upset with the other driver, drop back and give him/her space. At first you might find this difficult, as every bone in your body wants to 'show them' this is unacceptable behavior. Just do it! Let yourself know that while your new action might add on an extra one or two seconds' difference in time, it will make a massive difference to your health and well-being with lowered stress that will allow you to live longer. Besides, you don't know why the other person is cutting you off. They could be absent-minded, (aren't we all at some time or another?), or they might have an emergency.

Accept Without Prejudice

Don't let your own prejudices get in the way. For example, can you listen to an accent that is different to yours without prejudice, without thinking it's odd?

Accept Without Assumptions

Don't make assumptions about others. Assuming what other people are meaning from what they are saying, or assuming that other people are going to come to the same conclusions as you because your logic says so, can set you back. Instead ask what they mean and check your own assumptions. You will be surprised how people don't think what you think they think, and how much you will learn about them and yourself.

Accept Without Statements

Making statements can be interpreted as your point of view, and be contrary to another person's point of view. You could inadvertently steer the conversation in another direction by saying something like, "So that must have caused you a lot of anguish!" when in fact it didn't. Instead, ask a question: *"So what was that like?"* Be patient and give the other person time and space to formulate his or her own thoughts and expression. If you're not sure – ask!

Accept Without Interpretation

Similarly this holds true as with the above. Don't let your own ego, beliefs and life's experiences interpret what the other person is saying. Do not put your words or your interpretation of other people's statements into their conversation. Do not for example say, "You are raising an important issue" – it might not be an important issue! Ask a question first, *"Do you find that issue to be of importance to you?"* or, *"How important is that issue to you?"*

Do not say, "That must have been awful/wonderful for you" or, "I know how you feel!" or, "If I were in your situation, I would be frustrated too." The chances are that it was not awful/wonderful for them, and you don't know how they feel. It's just your interpretation. Instead ask a question, *"So how did you feel about that?"* or, *"So how was that experience for you?"*

Therapists know that if they give the answers or make supportive statements to their patients, it has nowhere near the strength of the patients saying the words themselves. When the patient hears him/herself talk and thinks about the words, he/she 'owns' the statement. Once the statement is owned by the patient, the therapist can move forward.

Obviously these guidelines are not cast in stone. If a person is jumping up and down with enthusiasm and there is excitement in the air, you don't have to confirm it with questions before you join in their excitement!

RULE #4: BE CURIOUS

Have you ever had someone respond to a problem you had asked them to help you resolve by them saying "You know what you should do . . . ." and you got upset about it, even if it made sense? You probably reacted to the fact that like most people, you don't like being told things. Even if the other person is right! The reason is that instant solution-focused responses to problems are based on little more than a scant piece of information about what is going on. It doesn't honor what action might have already been taken. You're being told what you should do and you don't like it because you don't feel a part of the dialogue. Even if you asked for help!

How do you think you would have felt if, instead of coming up with a solution, the other person had asked you questions to find out more about the problem – where it was coming from, how it was affecting you and what measures you had already taken to solve it – before coming up with some ideas? You probably would have felt involved, and as though the other person was respecting your intelligence and own process.

> *True listening happens when you're neither expecting nor judging.*
>
> – Yogi Amrit Desai

It's the same for your potential partners. So keep your comments, statements and solutions at bay until they are called for. Let the person you're talking with surface their own wisdom. What people say up front, and what appears to be face value, is usually not what it seems. Find out! They will respect you for it.

SUMMARY

The 4 Rules of Active Listening

1. Be Present	How?	Stay in the moment
		Good body language
		Give undivided attention
2. Be Acknowledging	How?	Good body language
		Feedback/summarize
		Verbal pauses
		Silence (silent = listen)
3. Be Accepting	How?	Without judgment
		Without prejudice
		Without assumptions
		Without statements
		Without personal interpretation
4. Be Curious	How?	Ask questions
		Be interested

CHAPTER 8

Knowing What To Listen For!

The answers to life's questions lie inside you
– all you need to do is look, listen and trust.

If the purpose of a business is to help other people solve problems, then doesn't it make sense to understand what is meant by problems? Problems *mean* different things to different people. For example, lack of time to fulfill dreams can be a problem for someone, can't it? Though in actual fact, the lack of time is not the problem. It's the *symptom* of something deeper that is causing the problem called 'lack of time!'

Getting behind the symptoms of people's problems is what it's all about. When you focus on exploring and *solving* the problems behind the *symptoms* of the problem, you replace the traditional route of having to talk about and present your business opportunity when you first meet with someone. And later, when you do talk about it, the correct features of the business opportunity that you will use to explain how the problem will be solved will come to you quite naturally. Why? Because the other person will have told you what to say. The next two chapters will demonstrate how you do this. You will learn to talk about solutions *after* you have understood what the real problem is. Grasp this concept close to your heart!

NEEDS AND PROBLEMS!

Needs and problems are essentially the same thing. If you have a need, then you have a problem, because the definition of a problem is simply *'the difference between what you've got and what you need.'* Conversely, if you have a problem, then you have a need: The need to resolve the problem!

You don't create needs. You can't. They are either there or they are not. You get to find out, even the forgotten and buried ones, by doing what? Asking questions and listening!

Needs usually arise because of something that's happening, or not happening, in your potential partner's environment at this *present time*. The depth of their desire to change or improve on their present circumstances will be driven by the facts, events and conditions that led them to this point in time, and how they feel about how it's affecting them. *How it's affecting them is what you need to listen for!*

Needs, or the resolution of problems are the driving force behind a person's willingness to talk with you, and learn about your solution, before making a commitment.

Your Objective

Your first destination in your 'Journey of Discovery' is to simply discover three things before you start talking about your solution. You need to discover:

1. Is there a problem to be solved?
2. Do they have a desire to change?
3. Do you have the right solution for them?

In chapter 6 on Current Reality, you discovered that by asking questions and exploring the facts about a person's present situation and how it's affecting them, you both get to see clearly where they are right now. From this point they will come to their first logical conclusion. They will either explore moving forward to get out of where they are, or stay where they are in their place of familiarity, even though it's uncomfortable.

Needs And Problems Come In Pairs

We've discovered before that the *degree* to which a person's motivation and commitment to change is in direct proportion to the *amount* of discomfort they feel about their present situation. People will explore and buy into your business opportunity to satisfy their needs and problems if the desire inside them is strong enough to do so. The key here is *the desire within them!* This desire is an emotion.

With that in mind and, as sure as night follows day, needs or problems come in pairs. *Outer Logical Needs (which deal with Facts) and Inner Emotional Needs (which deal with Feelings).*

Problems Come In Pairs

Outer Logical Needs
(Facts)

Inner Emotional Needs
(Feelings)

Let's start by exploring and understanding precisely what logical problems and needs are.

OUTER LOGICAL NEEDS

Whether you're talking with someone close to you or a complete stranger, as a skilled distributor and communicator, you can begin by finding out *who* your potential partner is and *what* they want.

WHAT DO PEOPLE WANT?

When you ask a person, *"What do you want?"* the answer you get will tend to be factual as the question is a factual one. Sometimes people will tell you what they want voluntarily without you asking. These outer logical problems and needs are expressed in many ways, such as the need for:

> More freedom
>
> More money
>
> More time

A residual income

Better health

Better results

Less stress

Less debt

Less cost

Fewer deadlines

Less politics

Less commute

Less work

Less effort

You might be tempted to think that responses like 'less stress and politics' are feelings and not facts! Don't be misled by this. Think about this expression. "The stress at the office with all the politics is just too much and I don't know what to do about it!" While this might be expressed with emotion, it doesn't alter the fact that you are only hearing facts – facts that the person is under a lot of stress and not very happy. If your response is to suggest how they need to get out of where they are and make a change, you know by now you're likely to be met with a lot of resistance.

FACTS ALONE HAVE VERY LITTLE PERSUASIVE OR EMOTIONAL POWER

Attempting to satisfy logical needs – the 'what' that a person is looking for can be tough work. And that is what the majority of distributors do. They only listen for and respond to the factual side of a problem. Facts such as, "I wish I had more money." or, "I wish I had better health." even, "I wish I had a different job." When hearing these logical needs, they immediately jump in with, "I can show you how to change that . . . ."

If you take this classical approach, you will waste time rattling off your presentation comprised of memorized features and advantages of your business opportunity, hoping that some of it sticks. It's like throwing mud at a wall. You don't know what clump is going to stick.

The result in most cases is that your prospective partner will back away and reject you and your solution. They resent it. You haven't respected the fact that *they have* the background history, *they know* what the circumstances were that brought them to this point, and *they know what*, if anything, they have done already about it. They need to be involved in this communication. Heed the ancient Chinese proverb: 'Involve me and I will understand.'

By not involving people and getting behind the facts, you can inadvertently offend them. And here is the tragic part: if you do, you won't even know it. People won't say anything. They will just psychologically withdraw. Think about how you felt, when someone told you what you should do! It can be irritating, can't it? And you probably either went quiet or responded a little aggressively.

You are also missing out on an opportunity to allow them to talk about how they are *feeling* about their present situation and how it's affecting them. Involve them! Ask them and they will tell you. They will also tell themselves. They will remind themselves that perhaps this is the time to change. They will sort this out internally. They do the work for you!

INNER PERSONAL NEEDS: IT'S FEELINGS THAT INSPIRE PEOPLE TO CHANGE!

Ask yourself, "Do people make major changes based on facts (logic) or emotions (feelings)?" The answer is that people make decisions based on feelings. *Logic is very rarely an internal persuader!* That's why distributors get rejected when only answering to facts. Responding to logic is talking from the head and rarely works. Responding to feelings is talking from the heart and this is where the relationship is made.

The inherent weakness in responding only to the logical side of needs and problems comes from not recognizing that the reason why someone has a need is based on circumstances *unique* to them! It's based on what *they* did to cause it, and how they feel about it at this moment! It is their inner self, their feelings and thoughts that will make the final decision whether to

> *Behind every fact there is a feeling if you care to find out*

change and take a look at your proposal. *Behind every fact there is a feeling if you care to find out.*

So the way you escape the monologue of having to present your business opportunity or tell your story is by asking questions to get behind the facts and find out how they feel about not having whatever it is they seek, and why they want what they don't have. (In the process you'll find that many people will surface problems that they have buried or forgotten they existed!)

Conversation is like an iceberg: 90% of an iceberg is submerged and only 10% is visible above the surface of the water. If you attempt to navigate to reach the 10% using only that 10% as your guideline, there is a good chance you'll end up like *The Titanic*! You'll be sunk by your lack of understanding of where the rest of the iceberg is. However, if you know where the depths and shallows are of the other 90%, you can navigate a safe passage over it.

In a similar way, 90% of someone's problem – the feelings, the emotions and the meanings – are submerged under the surface of most conversations. Even when these feelings and emotions are expressed, most distributors don't 'hear' them. They are too focused on listening for and answering the 10% 'above the surface' facts. Result? Their ship is sunk because they did not ask questions to find out what is lying beneath the surface!

In my experience, people regularly talk about their feelings using words like, "I'm not being fulfilled in my work," "I feel stuck!" "My lack of self-esteem at work is carrying over into my life." You just have to listen for these things and talk about them. This is very different from just addressing the external issues of wanting more money. There are deeper reasons for wanting more money. And when the time to change comes from a burning internal desire to do so, the commitment is permanent. And isn't this how you would like your downline to be? Forever? Isn't this the way you would like your customer base to be as well? Long term and committed?

"Many people assume without question that success is essentially material, that it can be measured in money, prestige or an abundance of possessions. These can certainly play a role, but having such things is no guarantee of success. Success achieved on the basis of struggle may bring good things to us, but the inner *fulfillment* we seek from those things will be lacking." – Deepak Chopra.

Facts belong to the world. Feelings belong to the individual.

So, look at the list of Outer Logical Needs again. You will hear these needs being expressed all the time. Add to this list all the things you hear people say they want. Keep adding to it. These are the facts you're listening for. However, *Facts belong to the world. Feelings belong to the individual.*

Let's look at this more closely:

BEHIND FACTUAL NEEDS THERE ARE FEELINGS

Having looked at what people want, it's just as important to discover <u>why</u> a person wants or doesn't want something. The *why* is the *emotional* or personal side of the needs equation. *It isn't what people want that is important, but the reason they want what they want!*

Now it's time to look at turning the *objective facts* you hear into *subjective reality!*

When people bring their current reality into the present and talk or think about what is missing in their lives or what they desire, it brings their feelings to the surface. These feeling are unique to each individual. We all respond and cope differently to similar situations.

Many people in sales never touch on these personal issues preferring to deal with the logical aspects of a problem. There is nothing wrong with this except we know people tend to make decisions based on emotions. Practically speaking from a sales perspective, if you don't touch the 'heart' button of understanding, chances are people will not do business with you or, if they do, won't stay all that long. This is a reason why people won't make a decision even if your solution from a logical viewpoint makes perfect sense.

Whether people look closely at your solution will depend on whether they feel you understand them and their unique subjective inner realities. This is important to know, because it is the sum of the *experiences, values, and beliefs* that form the core of their being. It is also important to the people you are talking with to know that you know.

So what are people looking for emotionally and the things you need to listen for?

INNER NEEDS/FEELINGS

To be listened to	To be acknowledged	To be among positive people
To be recognized	To be part of something	
To be heard		To have self-esteem
To be appreciated	To love and be loved	To have a sense of community
To be in control	To be fulfilled	
To be challenged	To be affirmed	To have a sense of security
To be validated	To be respected	
To be understood	To be liked	To have excitement

People are also looking for:

Achievement	Sense of safety	Stability
Power	Comfort	Harmony
Fun	Inner peace	Acknowledgment
Companionship	Assurance	Personal Satisfaction

Listen for these words and observe these feelings. Sometimes you will get the feelings and not necessarily the words. Connect their feelings to words if they don't give you the words. Do this by feeding back: *"I have a sense that you don't care for the experience of not being appreciated at work. Is that right?"* This is said like a caring question and the response you get will affirm your hunch or you will receive the precise feeling in their words.

Here's another example: *"When you say you're not getting the respect you want at work – what do you mean by that?"* Depending on the replies you can ask them, *"So how do you feel about that?"* You will learn how to extend these types of conversations in another chapter.

Listen for what *is not* being said as well as what *is* being said. Sometimes people will say something and you can sense through body language and/or the intonation of their voice that they don't really believe what they said. Discuss it! *"You don't seem too sure about that?" "I have a feeling that you'd like to be somewhere else if you could!"*

THE REAL NEED

So what's the real need that wants to be satisfied? It's the personal feeling needs for things such as assurance, security, self-esteem, respect, because that's what they don't get from their present experience. It's about how to change how their present and past experiences are affecting their body, mind and spirit. By asking about what happened and listening quietly, you allow your potential partner to subconsciously remind themselves of the consequences of what they are doing at the present, and how they feel about it. If it's uncomfortable enough, they will feel more inclined to move toward something else – and listen to your solution.

The key thing in this whole process is that instead of you telling your potential partners what they should do, they tell *themselves* what they should do by listening to themselves as they talk about what they want and why. They end up owning both the logical and feeling needs and will look seriously at your business opportunity because (1) it makes sense to do so, (2) no-one has ever bothered to understand them and what they are *really* looking for before, and (3) no-one has ever offered them an opportunity the same way as you!

People will explore and buy your solution not because they necessarily understand what it is or how it works, but because they feel you have listened to them and understood them as a unique person.

People buy solutions, goods and services, *for their reasons* not yours! They buy for what it will do for them, and how it will make them feel and how it will make them look to others and so on. People also buy *you*, because you are part of the *solution*.

If you appreciate, understand and can talk about this, the magnetic attraction it creates with your potential partner is profound. The field of energy of connection can only be understood once you experience it.

When you present your business opportunity later, you'll be able to demonstrate you've listened to their logical and emotional world of reality, so precisely, that you will feedback (in their words), the solution that will acknowledge exactly where they are coming from, what they are looking for, and why they want it, better than they can.

THE SKILLS

Here's a glimpse of how it works. This will be covered more in the later chapters on questions. You ask the question, *"What do you want?"* You listen to every word, as there are clues in their reply on which you ask more questions! You discuss what you've been told. You then ask another question, *"Can I ask you why you want that?"* You discuss this. Later, you ask, *"Why is that important to you?"* The response you get will give you the personal inner needs.

Looking at your Conversation Framework (Stage 2) you'll find the first question is a Needs Awareness Question. This will get the facts, (what they want). The second starts the transition toward the subjective reasons, and is another Needs Awareness Question. You might have to ask this question two or three times in different ways to get to the real truth. The third question, a Needs Development Question, will open up their feelings, (why they want it, and why it's important).

Here is a very brief example of this and I have notated the types of questions beside each one. We'll assume the other person has said. "I wish I had more money." (The lack of money being a symptom of a deeper problem. We now need to explore some history, to make the desire more meaningful in the present before exploring the future). Let yourself take the role of both people by answering the questions. Have a conversation with yourself. I do it all the time, especially before a meeting. It's called preparation!

> *"How long have you been without money?"* (Background Question)

> *"What does not having the funds prevent you from doing/having?"* (Needs Awareness Question)

> *"How do you feel about that?"* (Needs Development Question)

"How would having more money make your life different?"
(Needs Awareness Question)

"Is that important to you?" (Needs Development Question)

"How would that make you feel if you could do that?"
(Needs Development Question)

Ask people the questions they would ask themselves if they knew what to ask. Doing so will open up infinite avenues of thought and discussion. It will bring the other person closer to you and it will help them explore options they may not have considered before. When you later associate positive action steps with the options that will solve their problems, they will feel as though they are being helped and not imposed upon. Listen to the *heart* buttons not the *hot* buttons. The right buttons can be uncovered and explored through caring questioning. They are the essence of the person you are talking with. The Laws of Attraction will then be manifested and you can demonstrate the specific features of your business opportunity that will work for them.

Remember that 'Feelings are more powerful than facts, and even MORE powerful than thinking.' *You can't think without feeling! You can feel without thinking!* If you don't believe me, why is it that many voters on election night will vote for the other candidate at the last moment as they are checking their vote in the booth? Why is it someone will react suddenly to a loud noise in a quiet situation? Feelings are powerful. Listen to and find out the importance behind the answers to your factual questions. Listen for the feelings. People buy you and what you offer based on emotions. Find the need behind the need. The true needs will surface and your logical solutions will satisfy them.

So, before proposing the solution, understand what the present situation is and how the other person feels about it. It helps them to motivate themselves to change when the discomfort is great enough. As we have discovered, people make decisions emotionally and justify them logically!

Listen for both because you are going to use both sides of this information to present your solution. In the next chapter you will look at how to present what you have heard, linking the logical facts and the personal feelings to the advantages and benefits of your customized solution.

CHAPTER 9

Presenting Your Solution – Satisfying Needs

You don't need closing techniques for someone
who wants to make a change

In the last chapter you discovered that needs are caused by the circumstances that have led up to a person's present situation. You also learned how to listen to people's needs and discovered that needs and problems come in pairs (logical and emotional).

To successfully present your business opportunity when the time comes, you will be most effective when you can talk about and satisfy both the logical and personal needs you heard. In this chapter you will learn how to do that. You will learn that just as problems come in pairs, *so does your solution* and the way you present it!

SOLUTIONS COME IN PAIRS

The presentation of your business opportunity consists of finding the right features that will solve the logical side of a need, and explaining them as <u>Advantages</u>, and solving the personal side of a need by explaining the same feature as Benefits.

In my first few years of selling, one of my biggest challenges was that I never knew why people bought from me. I didn't know because I used presentation techniques that focused on selling the product not on understanding what someone wanted. It was all very hit or miss – and more miss than hit! While I got the 'Yeses' it took a lot of 'No's' and a lot of time and energy to get there. *It was a numbers game where quantity was sacrificed for quality.*

Today, I rarely get 'No's' because I can identify quite quickly what a person wants, why they want it, and whether they are prepared to make a change. From that I can determine whether my solution is likely to work for them. I can do this because I have already predetermined through my qualifying conversation that the person I'm talking with needs what I have and is open to listening. I don't have to say much about my solution, nor me unless I want to. (I've found the more I talk about me, the more I get into trouble!) During the dialogue, both of us at a point in time makes the decision to proceed with proposing that I might be able to help them. You can feel when the time is right. Trusting and using your intuition means you are letting the natural way take over.

I will then customize my presentation by feeding back my proposed solution in terms of its *advantages and benefits that will satisfy the specific logical and personal needs they have expressed to me.* All I'm doing is feeding back to them exactly what they told me they wanted.

You can do the same thing! It's hard for someone to turn you down if you demonstrate you understand what he or she wants, why they want it and, not only that, you can give them what they want.

STARTING WITH THE END IN MIND!

Before we look at what questions to ask, we will see how you are going to present your solution. Having an idea as to what to do when you get to the logical conclusion that you can be of help, will help you transition more easily. You will then see clearly the link between the needs you're listening to and how to explain and satisfy them.

FEATURES, ADVANTAGES AND BENEFITS

The key to presenting your solution can best be understood by considering the relationship between your prospective partner's *circumstances and logical and personal needs* on one hand, and your *solution*, (your business opportunity) which is comprised of *Features, Advantages and Benefits* on the other.

If you want to get to the heart of another person, spend time finding out the circumstances that are behind their problem, if they have one: Find out how it's affecting them, and *then* demonstrate how you can help by explaining your business opportunity in the form of talking about the *specific features* and their advantages and benefits that solves the problem. The words to remember are *specific features*. There is no point in talking about the feature residual income, for example, if a person's first priority is to move into a positive team environment, which is another feature! This will become clear as you progress through this chapter.

Look at the diagram carefully and see how this works. You will see how your solution, comprising features, advantages and benefits, satisfies the needs.

Before we go any further, let's clarify the definitions of three other phrases I have used:

CIRCUMSTANCES

The definition of circumstances is what has happened and/or what is happening, to cause a need or a problem.

A NEED OR A PROBLEM

A Need or a Problem is the difference between what your prospective partner has and what he/she wants.

A SOLUTION

A solution is an option that solves the problem, preferably by treating the cause. In this case it's your business opportunity.

FEATURES, ADVANTAGES AND BENEFITS

As I've mentioned before, your business opportunity is best explained by *presenting the advantages and the specific benefits of the features you have chosen to prescribe, after you have listened and found out what they are.*

Features, advantages and benefits are perhaps the most misunderstood and misused terms in selling! This chapter is devoted to giving you a clear description and understanding as to what they are, what they mean and how to use them to maximum advantage.

Here is an example of what I mean. Let's say you have had a conversation with someone. You have asked a number of questions, listened intently to the answers, have understood the problem, and you know the person is now open to listening to your presentation. During the conversation you discovered that residual income would be one of the features of your business opportunity that would be an answer for this person. You've proposed that you might be able to help and this is how you would present it at the 4th stage, The Presenting Stage, of your Conversation Framework:

"The residual income (feature) *from having your own business would take care of what you are looking for."*

"What this means to you is that in three or four years, the money you continually receive from your previous efforts means you won't have to be concerned about spending all your time making a regular income, and will free you to raise the funds to build that care center you were talking about." (Advantage)

"This will also allow you to get the fulfillment and recognition you said you were looking for and which is missing presently in your life and job!" (Benefit)

How do you know all of this and what to say? The other person told you! All you need to do is to explain about how the relevant features will solve the logical and personal problems.

Now, this presentation is very specific to a particular person and, of course, the only way you will know how to be that precise is to ask questions and listen to find out what their specific needs are. If you spoke with a different person and you discovered that the same feature could take care of their logical and personal needs, do you think you would describe the advantages and benefits in the same way? No, of course you wouldn't! Your description is customized to take into account what you have heard.

This is another reason why using dialogue and presenting your solution in precise terms is so much more effective than presenting sales pitches and telling stories at the beginning of a meeting. This natural way makes you very attractive in the eyes of your potential partner.

FEATURES

Definition: *A feature is a fact, data, information or characteristic about your solution (business opportunity).* Features are the elements that make your business opportunity what it is. It's a matter of choosing which features are most suited and relevant to helping the person you're talking with! Your business opportunity is comprised of hundreds of them. Here are a few features to think about. Add to this list and build your own arsenal of features and what they can mean.

> Be your own boss
> Residual income
> Time freedom
> Low start up cost
> Work when you want
> Work on your own
> Work as a team
> Tax deductibility
> Training given
> Support from successful people

Technical support

No inventory

No bookkeeping

No employees

Little paperwork

Company private/public

Company's been in business a long time – good track record

Company is financially sound!

UNDERSTANDING FEATURES

The first thing to understand is, *do not express features as benefits!* Features are the facts of your business opportunity, and on their own mean very little to most people. Talking about them in random isolation is like explaining something technical and talking about what it is, rather than *what it does*. It's like saying Network Marketing is about 'time freedom.' So what! Time freedom has to have some relevance to the person you told this to. It has to have meaning to that particular person if it is to have any effect. So it's important to express *why* your feature is important based on what you know the other people are looking for.

Features Statements very often are confused as Benefit Statements. Take the feature statement, 'You can work on your own' as an example. If you treat it as a benefit and said to someone early in a conversation, before you had found out very much about them, *"One of the benefits of having your own business is that you can work on your own,"* you stand a good chance of getting a blank stare.

The reason is that you're making an assumption! While *you* think it might be a benefit, does it mean the other person does as well? For example, it could be the person you're talking with couldn't think of anything worse than working on his/her own because of some bad experience perhaps! So where's the benefit in that?

On the other hand, if you had asked questions you might have discovered that he/she enjoyed working in a team with others. 'Working in a team' is another feature. Having found this out, you can later turn it into a benefit, such as, *"One of the benefits from working in a team is that you won't get that sense of loneliness you have in your present job that is making you feel depressed!"* How do you know you can say this? Because the other person told you what they didn't want and, therefore, what they *did* want!

Consider another example. What if you randomly talk about residual income to a prospective partner, and what they're looking for is a sense of community? Say he/she wants to work with people who are supportive because presently they are among negative people, which is making them feel a lack of self worth. Do you think there is any benefit talking about residual income? No! It remains exactly what it is – a feature or a fact. To mean anything a benefit has to be personal, to appeal to the person in question.

So 'working from home' or 'working in a team' or 'residual income' are merely features of your business opportunity, and talking about them as benefits will only have meaning if there is some personal context to it.

Here are some more examples. Perhaps you find yourself making these statements at random:

> *"Our company is established. It has been around for nine years."*
> *"You have the freedom to work when you want!"*
> *"You can start your own business with little money down!"*
> *"Our training is the best!"*

So what? What does this mean to the person you're talking with? To be effective, features must have context with what another person is looking for! If you do make statements like these and the response you get is low, now you know why! These statements are *feature statements*. They are *not* benefit statements! As such, feature statements mean very little to most people when expressed in isolation.

So be aware of this and steer away from *randomly* talking about features as though they were benefits. It's another reason why presenting your solution before understanding what another person wants can raise objections!

TURNING FEATURES INTO PERSONALIZED ADVANTAGES AND BENEFITS!

The key to talking about features is to talk only about the specific features that respectively solve the logical and personal problems. So if you discover a person is looking to make more money in their spare time, then working part-time is a feature you can use. In the next chapters, you will learn how to ask the right questions to find out all the information you need to do this.

Now compare the list of logical needs and problems that people have in chapter 8, with the features that were previously listed. You'll see that some of the features are the specific answers to the logical needs!

So make it a point to understand how the specific individual features solve specific individual problems. When you hear someone talking about wishing they had more time to spend with their kids, talk about it with them. Don't automatically assume that the 'time' feature is going to be the main one to use.

Instead, ask them what is preventing them from getting the time. Ask them how they see themselves resolving the problem. They might reply that they see the answer as having their own part-time business but don't know what to do because they don't have any experience. Even though a feature of your business opportunity is that a new distributor can be 'trained' to get the right level of experience, instead of blurting out, *"You don't need any experience because we'll train you!"* – ask what specific experience they think they need.

They might tell you that they don't have any bookkeeping experience and that they don't have any space for inventory. Can you see the picture becoming larger and more specific? The problem becomes clearer and consequently so will how you present your solution. When you offer how you can help, you simply talk about the specific concerns they have brought up and link them to the *correct* features that will take care of the problem, such as time freedom, minimal bookkeeping, training given, inventory is kept at the company's location, being your own boss.

If you had started immediately telling them they didn't need any experience you would miss learning the specific concerns. This is why people raise objections. So let the other person eliminate the objections themselves and make it easy for yourself. Ask questions and from the answers tailor your presentation each time to the specific needs of the person with whom you are talking. Spend the time talking about needs and concerns. The longer you spend, the more *both of you* learn. *Go slow, to go fast*!

And don't forget to ask them if that sounds like something that might take care of what they want. Get confirmation. Remember, when they say it, it's true!

FEATURES ARE THE LIFEBLOOD OF YOUR BUSINESS

Features then are what you use to solve problems. Remember them. Many are self-evident, and you hear and talk about them all the time when talking with your associates. Use them selectively. They are the lifeblood of your business.

As I mentioned before, there are many features and sub-features that comprise your business opportunity. Look through all your company material and brochures and dig them out and keep a list of them. You actually don't need to memorize all of them, but you never know when they may come in handy!

An Example Of Personalizing Your Presentation

Let's assume you've been interviewing someone and you discovered relevant needs that indicated to you residual income would be a great feature to talk about.

When you come to describe and demonstrate your solution, in terms of its features, advantages and benefits, this is how you can present it. Begin with the feature first:

"One of the aspects (features) about our business, that could give you what you're looking for, is your ability to make a residual income!"

It's important you don't stop here. Don't leave it up to the other person to work it out. They could ask themselves "So what does this mean to me?" And you probably wouldn't know it, because they wouldn't tell you, for not wanting to appear ignorant, or for a million other reasons that are personal to them. Eliminate potential gulfs in your communication by making sure you follow up with explaining the advantages and the benefits of your business opportunity, to demonstrate you have a clear understanding.

Advantages

Let's look at what an advantage is before continuing with our presentation example.

Definition: *An Advantage illustrates HOW the right feature* **satisfies the logical needs** *of your prospective partner's particular problem.* An Advantage is what your solution means to your potential partner.

An advantage could be:

- Something your prospective partner doesn't have or use.
- Something your competitors don't have.

- Something your prospective partner hasn't thought about.

Having heard the needs of the other person, you repeat the needs back to them in the *positive form* as an advantage that answers their need and supports your solution. Don't assume your potential partner will work it out for his/herself. Just because he/she might have said what they were looking for earlier doesn't mean they will automatically make the link between the feature and what it means to them. Make sure they understand by repeating it back. Let's continue with the presentation:

"One of the aspects (features*) about our business, that could be what you're looking for, is your ability to make a residual income!"*

"What this means to you is that (1) you'll have more money to go on vacation while you're in good health, (advantage*) because (2) you won't have to pay into that expensive disability plan.* (advantage) *The residual income will replace your payments into it and also pay you should you be unfortunate enough to be ill.* (advantage)*"*

Logical Needs Fulfilled! (More money, less cost, more freedom, more financial security.)

This is how you talk compellingly about features in terms of their advantages. It demonstrates understanding and that you have listened.

Remember and use these terms to start your advantage statements:

"What this means to you is . . . ."
"This will help you solve the problem by . . . ."
"This will be important to you because . . . ."
"You'll like this because . . . ."
"Others find this useful because . . . ."
"This will be helpful to you because . . . ."
"This is an important point for you . . . ."

"You'll find this of value because . . . ."
"Because of this feature you can . . . ."
"When this happens you can expect . . . ."
"This means you can . . . ."

"SO WHAT?"

Just in case you might be tempted to think that the advantage statement is a benefit one, don't stop here! While for some people, the advantages (solving the logical needs) might be enough for them to become a partner with you, make sure and give more of a personal reason for them to be inspired to take action. Go the extra step and explain how your opportunity can satisfy the internal personal need by explaining how the feature as a benefit will make them feel!

BENEFITS

Research shows that if you express your solution in terms of benefits, you will increase your sales by nearly a third. People remember the benefits, because they are personal. This is especially useful if the sales process takes more than one step, and/or others are involved. Your prospective partners will talk benefits to each other because it *has to do with feelings – personal feelings*. Very rarely will they talk about facts!

Definition: *A benefit illustrates how the right feature and its advantages satisfies the inner personal needs, feelings and values of your prospective partner.* A benefit is how your solution will allow your potential partner to *feel* as a result of the logical need being satisfied.

You discovered earlier that people will make a change from what they are doing now to something else, based on an inner desire to do so. With this in mind, your prospective partner will view your solution more favorably when you reinforce *why* they would want to consider a change. By talking about your solution in terms of their reasons, not yours, you make a very <u>compelling</u> offer.

Consider this: people don't buy opportunities, goods and services. They buy because of:

- How they think your solution will make them personally feel
- What they think your solution will do for them
- How they think your solution will make them look to others.

Consider these examples to illustrate the above:

Jane doesn't want to work from home and have the residual income just because it will give her the time and financial freedom. (features) She wants it to have more quality time with her kids because they are the most important people in her life (advantage), and it means she no longer has to feel desperate about missing their formative years. (benefit)

Bob doesn't want more time (feature) just to play golf. He wants it because he can now spend more time with his friends (advantage) and feel reconnected and no longer frustrated and sad because they were drifting away. (benefit)

This is an example of hearing and responding to the 2nd principle, which is listening to what is being *meant*, and not *just* what is being said!

THE PERFECT PRESENTATION!

Continuing with, and taking the presentation example to its ultimate conclusion, this is how you explain the benefits of residual income, your chosen feature – residual income:

"One of the aspects (features) *about our business, that could be what you're looking for, is your ability to make a residual income!"*

"What this means to you is that (1) you'll have more money to go on vacation while you're in good health, (advantage) *be-*

cause (2) you won't have to pay into that expensive disability plan. (advantage) *The residual income will replace your payments into it and pay you should you be unfortunate enough to be ill.* (advantage)"

"This will allow you to feel good about being able to join your friends once again in Europe every year (benefit), *and not feel as though your are losing touch with them.* (benefit) *You also won't have to worry needlessly about the consequences* (benefit) *of not being insured."*

"Does this sound what you're looking for?"

Personal Needs Fulfilled! (Pleasure, no-risk, safety, respect, pride, self-esteem.)

Important Note: Whenever you can, end your statements, answers and summations with a question. This stops the conversation from possibly hanging in the air. It also asks for confirmation that this is what your prospective partner is looking for.

So that is an illustration of how you can effectively present your solution. In doing so you satisfy the internal and external needs that you learned about in chapter 8. (You can appreciate the preceding presentation is unique to a particular person. It will change depending on what you hear.)

Remember, the more you speak in terms of specific features, advantages and benefits when you present your solution, the stronger the meaning and impact it will have on your prospective partner. In the above example, some of the internal motivators you could have recognized, and be satisfying, are the need for:

- *Safety and security,* because he/she doesn't have to worry about the expense or consequences of being in Europe.

- *Self-esteem* is returned. Self-esteem that was lost when he/she couldn't keep up with his/her friends' travel plans through lack of finances.

- *Pride,* because he/she can afford to be with his/her friends in Europe.
- *Self-Respect* and respect from the friends for the same reason.

Talking about benefits touches the 'heart' of your potential partners. It's what makes people tick. It appeals to and acknowledges their subjective reality. Sometimes this reality is hidden from them until someone like you 'touches' them and 'exposes' it. By listening for and by directly and indirectly addressing these issues, you help people identify what it is they really seek.

To get a picture of what the whole process looks like, follow the flow on the diagram. You'll notice that the Outer Logical Needs (facts) are satisfied by your business opportunity (your solution), comprised of the right feature(s) that are explained as an advantage!

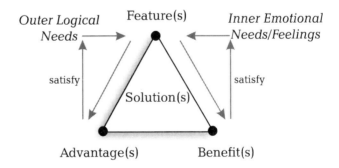

The same thing happens at the same time with the Inner Emotional/Personal Needs side (feelings). This need is satisfied by you tagging on to the end of your presentation, an explanation as to how the same feature takes care of the personal feelings.

It's through dialogue, by *Asking Questions*, *Listening* and finally *Presenting*, that you and your potential partner reach a mutual understanding. They will give you all the factual and internal needs you need to put together a perfect and effective presentation. If there is a problem to be solved, and your prospective partner can see, feel and believe the features, advantages and benefits gained from your solution, they will buy it. Your job is to help them see it.

TAILOR YOUR PRESENTATION

Tailor your presentation differently to each prospective partner. This is not a 'canned pitch.' This is not guesswork. This is precise and accurate and based on all the facts and feelings you heard, saw and felt.

When you finally *present* your solution to satisfy your prospective partner's needs, for maximum effect, make sure you focus your *presentation* on the following:

- Features you have chosen in your solution that are relevant to solving the problem, such as *more time by working at home.*
- Advantages that are linked to solving the logical needs, such as *being with the kids more often.*
- Benefits that are linked to satisfying the internal needs such as not feeling depressed because they won't be missing the best years of their kids' lives!

Use these phrases whenever you can to remind you to focus on the logical and emotional reasons for the buying decision.

- *"What this means to you . . . ."* To tie back the advantages (logic), to the logical need, and,
- *"Which will allow you . . . ."* To tie back to the dream (feelings) to the personal need.

- *"Does that take care of . . . ?"* Confirms that you and your prospective partner agree.

Only use the features that fit the needs you uncover during your Discovery Process. You have many features from which to choose. Only use those wanted by your prospective partner. And, remember, different prospective partners will need the same features for different reasons. The process of presenting will be addressed again as we continue using the Conversation Framework over the remaining chapters.

Part IV

Principle #3
How To Ask The Right Questions
At The Right Time

Chapter 10:
The Art Of Asking Questions

Chapter 11:
The Connecting Stage

Chapter 12:
The Discovering Stage

Chapter 13:
The Transitioning Stage

CHAPTER 10

The Art Of Asking Questions

I keep six wise serving men. They taught me all I knew. Their names were, WHAT and WHY and WHEN and HOW and WHERE and WHO. – Rudyard Kipling

SIX SERVING MEN, SIX QUESTIONS – THE MOST VALUABLE TOOLS IN YOUR DISTRIBUTOR KIT!

Asking good questions is the most powerful tool for improving your relationship and sales results. Your sales brochures, websites, videos and audio tapes, or anything else you use, turn from being sales 'crutches' (where you are hoping that these items will sell your prospective partner), to being tools of 'support,' to be used when and if you need them. Giving away tapes, brochures and telling people to go to a website don't create relationships. People talking with people do!

A relationship is born from a desire to understand someone. In return there will be a desire to understand you. Personalizing your discussion around what is important to others will do this for you.

ASKING QUESTIONS TO DISCOVER AND EXPLORE

You have already learned how to listen, why you listen and what to listen for. In the following chapters you will discover how to ask the questions to discover and explore the circumstances that causes the problems that people have as well as the circumstances surrounding the problem. It's through dialogue with your potential partner, by asking questions and listening, that you reach a mutual understanding of all these elements that will enable you to formulate a successful presentation.

Use questions wisely. From previous chapters you know they will allow you to discover *if* there is a need, what a person wants, why they want it and how it's affecting them by not having it. They will also let you find out what they've done about it, what would they do about it, whether it's important enough for them to change and much more!

The diagram below will help you see this:

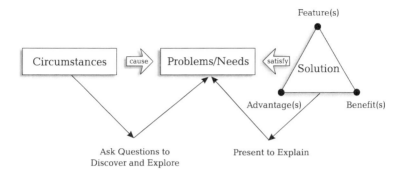

'POWERFUL QUESTIONS GET POWERFUL ANSWERS!'

Asking questions is sometimes referred to as 'The high art of selling.' When you *ask factual* and *feeling* questions, the answers you get are the signs on the signposts on the road to your first destination. What is this first destination? To discover if they have a problem and, if they do, do they have a desire to solve it, and to see if you can help them. That's your first destination. *Focus not on making the sale. Focus on whether there is a sale to be made in the first place.*

As you listen, the correct features of your solution will become obvious to you. As they do, you can explore whether they are possibly the right ones by asking more questions. For example, if you hear a mother feeling anguish over the fact that she cannot give her children the quality time they deserve because she has to go to work, an obvious feature of your business opportunity is that she can 'work from home.'

Focus not on making the sale. Focus on whether there is a sale to be made in the first place.

Asking more questions will surface perhaps more compelling features to talk about. Build your questions around the history of what is presently happening: What her present work is, the hours she is working, whether she has thought about what kind of work she would do at home, and how important or urgent is it to start making a change, and so on. As she answers your questions she subconsciously reinforces her desire to work from home. It also gives you the information on how to later present the correct features of 'working at home,' etc., in terms of their advantages and benefits that are specific to this person.

Don't forget she will have the answers to what she wants! It's just that she might not have the right solution. You might! And, by asking questions, you will know what to present when the time comes to do so!

Look at what good questions do:

Questions Gather Information
They uncover problems and explore if there is a need.

Questions Enable You To Understand The Priorities
Questions enable you to understand the priorities of each need.

Questions Analyze And Diagnose
Questions analyze and diagnose your potential partner's needs/problems and their causes that allow you to know what to say when you present your solution.

Questions Are Like A Stethoscope
They will reveal to you the internal *beat* of the other person. *Good questions reveal your own internal beat as well.* They reveal your intent – your purpose – which is to help people find the right solution. The positive energy you create subconsciously helps your potential partner recognize the value of who you are and what you offer – even before you offer it!

Questions Involve The Other Person

They fill the mind of, and actively involve, your potential partners. It makes them feel part of the process. When they answer you, and you listen and respond to their answers by asking additional questions to gain more understanding, they feel their ideas, comments and concerns are honored and validated.

Questions Internally Motivate The Person You're Talking With

The results you're looking for are in the answers to your questions. Answering your questions is a very powerful internal motivator for people. It makes them automatically feel they want to take action. You don't have to do anything to externally motivate people. Just ask questions and listen! *You can ask and listen people into changing!*

Questions Put You In Control

Control – not for power and manipulation, but for you to easily keep the conversation on track.

Questions Paint A Picture

The answers to your questions allow your potential partners to paint a picture of everything they want, or don't want, and why they want it, or don't want it. If you listen, *you* get to see their picture.

Questions Are For The Other Person

While you get to see their picture, who else gets to see it? The person answering the questions! Their answers can give them a different perspective, and can motivate them to redraw their picture to make it better or bigger. They learn directly and indirectly from their own answers as they move along the conversation of discovery with you.

During the journey they can decide for themselves if they want to make a change. You empower people to get in touch with their feelings about their present circumstances, and allow them the choice to take action that will come from a deep internal desire to do so, not from a temporary external motivation that occurs from manipulation.

A good doctor does a similar thing: He/She does not give the answers to the patient without first asking questions and listening, because it would be the doctor's answer, not the patient's. The patient answering the questions knows the circumstances and will discuss them. Their symptoms become clear to them. They might not know what the solution is to their problems, but the doctor will. And the patient feels part of the process! The patient is more likely to accept and take the prescription.

It's the same for you. People will discuss their circumstances with you as a trusted advisor. They will work with you to iron out their concerns. For many, it may be *the first time they've 'seen' their picture in a long time*. They get to see problems they never thought they had. It makes them more curious about working out how to move forward. At the end they are more likely to look at and accept y*our* prescription!

As you ask questions about what they would do if they could, you will hear comments like:

> "Oh I gave up on that a long time ago!"
> "That was a dream I once had and will never realize."
> "Interesting you should ask that, I would like to, but I'm afraid it's not possible so I don't even go there any more!"

On hearing these comments, you can ask, *"Ah! But what if you could and there was nothing stopping you."* Having built the rapport of trust, you will hear the real dreams declared. As most people don't see the world as it is, and see the world as they are, their answers to your questions give them a broader view of life.

On hearing someone declare what they would do – don't immediately respond with a, *"If I could show you how to do that, would you be interested?"* question. This puts the focus immediately back on you and your agenda and is a turn-off for most people. Be patient – ask more questions.

Questions Open Up Consequences

Questions open up consequences: The consequences of making, or not making, certain decisions. If it's obvious to you that a person is going to make a decision about something that is not going to serve them, you can ask questions that will help them rethink their actions.

Questions Create Value In You And What You Represent

The way you create value in you, who you are, and later what you have to offer, is by asking the right questions at the right time, and listening. People buy you first on the strength of how much you understand them.

For example, let's say you have a booth at a trade show and someone comes up to you and asks you to tell them about your business opportunity. Instead of telling them what you think it's all about in the classical way, find out why they asked. First of all, briefly answer the question with an advantage statement, such as:

"Well, what we do is help people set up their own home-based businesses so that they can start taking care of themselves and their families once again"

Then you would immediately follow up with a question, such as:

"Is this something you're looking for?"

Don't assume they are looking to start their own business. Find out and qualify them. Whether they answer 'yes' or 'no' doesn't matter.

If they say 'yes' then you continue asking questions as to what they are doing presently, how long they have been doing it, what they like and don't like about it, how they feel about it, and so on. If their discomfort with what they are doing is great enough, most people will look seriously at changing it for something else. This is what I mean – that questions create value in you and what you represent!

If they say 'no', still ask the same questions. You'll be surprised how quickly you'll find that people don't always mean what they say. There are many truths. The correct one sets them free.

Questions Reduce Anxiety

For the both of you! For you, because the focus is off of you – and for the other person, because they are talking about themselves!

Questions Clear Up 'Fuzzy Thinking'

They ensure you and your potential partner share the same understanding.

Questioning Opens Lines Of Communication

Asking questions of clarification can make sure that everyone is on the same track.

Questions Allow You To Plant Your Own Ideas

You can make suggestions such as:

"What if you were to take this approach . . . (describe your idea.) Would that make it easier for you?"

Questions Let You Address Concerns

When faced with another person's concerns, about selling for instance, instead of handling them like an objection, you *address* them by asking questions to get behind the concern so that you can understand it and jointly come up with a solution. Using dialogue and the Conversation Framework will enable you to do this!

TURNING YOUR KNOWLEDGE INTO QUESTIONS

Instead of making statements, use the power of asking questions. Instead of telling people about what you know, ask questions that will uncover and explore what they know about the subject first.

If you tell people outright your solution, *you* can be the one who ends up owning the problem *and* owning the solution. The result being that your potential partner will be less attached to it than if *they* were part of the process and *they* owned it. *Use your knowledge to ask questions.*

Use your knowledge to ask questions.

Let's suppose you know that social security pensions are in jeopardy because there will be more people who will be entitled to them than those who can support the plan. Instead of stating what you know, you could open up a dialogue by asking, *"Have you ever considered how we will be financially affected when we retire with fewer people putting less money into social security?"*

Here are some more examples that will get your mind into a question mode and not a telling mode:

- Instead of saying that your business opportunity will give people financial freedom, ask them if financial freedom is important to them.

- Instead of telling people you know how they can get out of their present job and start working for themselves, ask if they have ever *thought* about working for themselves?

- Instead of saying that your opportunity will give people residual income, ask them what they would do if they had a steady income that came in without them having to work for it anymore.

QUESTIONS COME FROM TWO SOURCES

There are two sources of questions available to you:

1. The ones you learn in this book to start, continue, and end conversations.

2. The ones you ask, based on the answers you get to your previous questions.

Generally, you can take it as a given that the second source is more powerful. These questions are in response to what your potential partner is telling you how they are thinking, feeling and wanting. Also it's polite, and most people like it that you have shown an interest in them and, if you want to be pragmatic about it, *they* have the background, and y*ou* need to tap into it!

THE CONVERSATION FRAMEWORK

Let's revisit the Conversation Framework again and now look precisely at the types of questions you can ask, when to ask them and why you ask them!

While it might appear there are a lot of different types of questions to memorize, it will soon come as second nature to you. Continual practice is the key. Your success will exponentially increase with the improvement in the quality of your questions and the quality of your listening.

Learn the phrases in the different stages. Make them your own. Learn from what people say to you. Prepare and rehearse your conversations. Plan what you are going to say. Practice having conversations with yourself! Be patient. Always come back to the 4 guiding principles: These are the rails that will keep you on track.

Whatever you're feeling is what you're resonating, and whatever you're resonating is what you're attracting.

Over a short time you will reframe your old responses that don't work for you. Even if you implement only a little at first, people will notice and the natural laws of attraction will start to take effect. *Whatever you're feel-*

ing is what you're resonating, and whatever you're resonating is what you're attracting.

The next chapter will look at the various ways you can start conversations that will:

- Immediately draw people to you, by putting the focus on them.

- Help people feel comfortable about talking about themselves, so they will reveal their own inner world of reality to you.

Remind yourself of the five stages of the Conversational Framework and use it as your roadmap to make the attraction of the 4 Natural Selling® principles work for you.

Natural Selling® Conversation Framework
The Discovery Process

1 Connecting Stage

CONNECTING QUESTIONS
Demonstrates your intent. Puts focus on other person.

2 Discovering Stage

BACKGROUND QUESTIONS
Finds the present situation - the basic facts.

NEEDS AWARENESS/ DEVELOPMENT QUESTIONS
Explores needs/problems if any. *What* your customer wants.
Explore circumstances causing the needs. Why your customer wants it.
Reveals the correct features, advantages and benefits to solving the problem.

CONSEQUENCE QUESTIONS
Expands on the problems.
Makes the need more urgent.
Explores consequences of making a wrong decision.

SOLUTION QUESTIONS
Involves your customer and their ideas.
Reveals and strengthens the benefits of solving the problem.

QUALIFYING QUESTIONS
Confirms if other person is ready to take action.

3 Transitioning Stage

TRANSITION QUESTIONS
Opens the door to presenting your solution.

4 Presenting Stage

SUMMARY AND AGREEMENT
Confirms the correct solution. Presents the specific features, advantages
& benefits of the solution that solves the problem and satisfies the needs.

5 Committing Stage

COMMITMENT QUESTIONS
Helps other person to commit or take the next steps.

For a free LARGER copy of this chart, go to
www.NaturalSelling.com/charts.html

CHAPTER 11

Stage 1: The Connecting Stage – Starting Effective Conversations

Strangers are friends we haven't met yet

Every day you are faced with opportunities to connect with people. They can either be instigated by yourself, through calling known contacts, calling leads, making cold calls, talking with strangers, placing ads in the media, or they can happen by chance such as being introduced to someone by a friend or by someone asking you a question. It's *your* opportunity to have a close look into another person's 'world of reality' and discover if you can be of service.

This chapter will give you ways of *starting* the process of discovering, by giving you the tools to effectively open conversations by putting the focus firmly on people with whom you're speaking.

SETTING THE STAGE!

The first words you say, or the first questions you ask, can compel people to be drawn to you and feel comfortable enough to open up to you if you do it correctly. To create a good first impression, start asking interesting questions the moment you start a conversation. 'Connecting questions' will achieve this for you because they will:

- Allow you to talk with people without the fear or anxiety normally associated with selling, or wondering what to say! When you put the focus on the other person and immediately establish rapport, you don't have to find something of commonality to discuss. The common bond you have is the one thing they are interested in – themselves and their present situation.

- Allow you to see, feel, and hear the positive change in people's responses to you and the positive changes in your own feelings.

- Allow you to be comfortable, as well as effective, with what you're doing. When y*ou're* comfortable, and feeling self-assured, this manifests itself to others with whom you are speaking. They feel comfortable and self-assured. *Focusing on the other person will decrease your anxiety!*

- Set the stage for continuing to ask questions throughout your Discovery Process.

- Establish a relationship before you even start talking about you.

- Make you appear friendly, professional and competent.

- Immediately create value in you and what you represent.

- Allow you to control the process from the beginning. Being in control means being in control of yourself and the conversation. This allows you to be open and guide the conversation to a logical conclusion.

So whether someone starts talking with you, or you call them, it's imperative you start by finding out what they want and why they want it from the very beginning!

FOUR WAYS A CONVERSATION CAN START

Apart from the greeting and a "Hello" or a smile, there are four possible ways a conversation can start:

1. You make a statement.
2. They make a statement.
3. You ask a question.
4. They ask a question.

YOU MAKE A STATEMENT

When you make a statement you express an opinion – your own. In many cases, your statement doesn't matter. It's only your opinion. You might also be called on to back it up which could lead you into discussion and debate and away from dialogue. Ask yourself, does your opinion when unasked for, matter to most people? Probably not! You might want to consider keeping your statements to yourself!

THEY MAKE A STATEMENT

When someone else makes a statement they are expressing their opinion – and their own opinion carries weight because it's coming from their 'world of reality.' Whether you agree with them or not doesn't matter. It's an opportunity for you to acknowledge the statement and to ask questions that will open up what was behind it. As you discovered in the section of this book about listening, you don't have to *agree* with someone to *listen* to them to discover what they're thinking and why they're thinking this way.

YOU ASK A QUESTION

When you ask a question, the focus mostly goes on to the other person. They feel it and it makes them feel important, especially if it comes from the heart and with good intent. Start connecting with people by starting with a question.

THEY ASK A QUESTION

The traditional way of responding to someone's question is to answer it at face value and sometimes go into presenting mode to back it up. Think carefully before you do that! Make sure you understand the questions behind the question (if there are any!) Here is a formula to help you to find out and escape the trap of telling before you know what to tell!

- Understand the question. (Ask for clarification if you need to.)
- Acknowledge the question.
- Ask a question after you have answered it!

If you don't understand the question – ask for clarification. Don't pretend you know what they meant as you will end up taking a lonely journey down a one-way street called dead end!

Acknowledging a question is different than answering it! Acknowledging it could be as simple as saying, *"I'd love to reply to that and, before I do, let me understand why you are asking it."* In this way, you end up putting the focus on the other person, which makes you shine because most people love talking about themselves, and you get the questions behind the questions!

EXPECT POSITIVE RESPONSES

You are what you think – you get what you expect. Negative expectations come from fear. Your thoughts can be self-limiting. Freedom comes when you let go of your attachment to fear.

Despite what you think, people are not ready to bite your head off when you say you are involved in Network Marketing! (As a side note: personally, I wouldn't bring it up unless it was relevant to the conversation or someone asked. The reason is that Network Marketing is basically an industry and form of distribution. Consider this: If you were a doctor and someone asked you what you did, would you say, "I'm a doctor in the medical industry?" Probably not. It doesn't make sense! You would just say, "I'm a doctor." So why bring up Network Marketing? Why not say, "I have my own business as an independent distributor?" Be assured I'm not suggesting you do this to hide from having to say it. Many people I've met have either not known what Network Marketing is or have heard great things about it. I'm suggesting that the world is not always as you see it. Feel, think, see, and do things that will serve you better.)

Most people do not think what you think they think. However, if you insist that they do – then they will. They can't help it. And nor can you, because your thinking resonates in the energy of your words and the way you say your words. If you want people to change their response to you, change your thoughts, change your words. I was reminded of this by a Buddhist monk a few years ago who explained that, in the Buddhist tradition, everything begins with a feeling or a thought, and to make sure you:

> *Watch your thoughts: They become your words.*
>
> *Watch your words: They become your actions.*
>
> *Watch your actions: They become your habits.*
>
> *Watch your habits: They become your character.*
>
> *Watch your character: It becomes your destiny.*

So, if you want to change your destiny, change your thoughts. Realize your own fears are just that – your own fears. If you transfer your fear to another person because of your thoughts and words, they will mirror it back to you. Whatever you put out, you get back!

This is why the intent behind the first principle of Natural Selling's® of 'helping others solve their problems' is important to understand and absorb. By realizing the reason you do what you do is to help others, and continually learning how to get better at doing it, you will, over time, release all your fears because your thoughts will change.

THINK IT – DO IT – BE IT – THINK IT

If you wait to be good, you'll wait forever. The only way you can be good is to start now and *do it*. Give yourself permission and the freedom to fail occasionally. Letting go of the need to get it right all the time, frees you from the fear of failure. It doesn't matter. What matters is that you do it. Obstacles, barriers, and hurdles along the road are merely stepping stones to success. So *do it* and *be it*.

Being it is the embodiment of everything. Be the person you want to be. Observe others you would like to be like and become the parts of what you like best about them. And here is something to help remind you of this. To amusingly paraphrase a Taoist expression and bring into more modern times:

To be is to do – Jean-Paul Sartre
To do is to be – John Mill
Do-be-do-be-do – Frank Sinatra

ONE STEP AT A TIME

The only way to influence the future is to do it in the present moment. Take effective mini steps to move you forward to achieving your goals and your higher purpose more rapidly. By this I mean, when you start to use the principles and methods in this book, take one step at a time. For example when you complete this chapter, immediately begin to use the phrases you learned and do nothing more than observe how people respond to you in a more positive way. If the conversation doesn't turn out the way you would like, or you're not sure what to say next, let it go! Just look for and feel good about the difference in attitude that people will have for you. Actually, it's a difference that has always been there, except you never saw it before because of 'Where you were.' *Changing your approach will change their response!*

Taking small steps like this, and feeling the positive results of people responding to you will encourage you to take bigger ones. As you do so and you actually see and feel the positive results manifested by your new action – through your new words and phrases – you *will* feel better about yourself. Those new feelings of well-being will further feed and nourish the inner mind – the subconscious – which will then resurface into the conscious again and automatically give you the right words to use each time. Words that have strength and conviction, words of intent and words that are coming from a subconscious reference point of abundance. By being outwardly abundant, the abundance you are looking for will flow quite freely to you – if you let it.

YOUR SOLUTION IS UNIQUE IN THE WORLD OF BUSINESS OPPORTUNITIES

Finally, take a moment to appreciate what you have. Take a look at what you're doing, what your solution *means*, and *why* it is so valuable – if you haven't discovered it already. *You* have a signed document with your Network Marketing Company that gives you the rights to sell their products, services or business opportunity, *and* the rights to find others to sell it for you.

Here's the thing that differentiates what you've got from most other businesses. *You also have the rights to sell those rights to someone else who can do the same thing!* That's like having a McDonald's franchise and having the rights to sell McDonald's franchises to others!

That's unique, powerful and valuable, and puts you in the driver's seat. So take the position of having as many *quality* interviews as possible to find the *right* people to join you – motivated people who want to make a change in their lives. It doesn't take many people to build a solid, self-sustaining, self-motivated and loyal organization.

The time and energy you spend with them on the front end is well invested. They will stay with you and do whatever is necessary. Your attrition rate will dramatically reduce, and your new associates will help you reach your objectives as you help them reach theirs.

CONNECTING QUESTIONS AND THE PROCESS OF CONNECTING

With practice you will automatically get better and respond with the right words and right phrases for each situation. As you progress, you'll notice conversation patterns emerging and they will come to you with ease – especially if you *become* what you are doing.

What you learn here is not set in stone. Vary the phrases and words to suit your own style and personality and situation. If the words don't suit you, change them. Look for the intent behind the questions and make them work for you.

EFFECTIVE CONVERSATION STARTERS

Let's look at the various ways of how you can effectively connect and start conversations with people by turning the focus onto them.

HOW TO INTRODUCE YOURSELF AND MAKE AN IMMEDIATE IMPACT!

I would like to share with you a powerful and very flexible communications tool that can be used in a variety of situations. It's called the Personal Introduction.

When people ask you, "What do you do?" – how do you normally reply? Do you answer with the title of your job description? Such as, I'm a nurse, I'm an office administrator, I sell health products, I work with a nutritional marketing company, I'm in the health and wellness industry, or whatever you *do*? What does this mean to the person who asked you? Not much. It tells very little about y*ou!*

One of the most magnetic ways I know of attracting people to you, is not to tell people *what* you do, but let them know *how* what you do, *helps* other people. And this is where the personal introduction comes into its own! It has a variety of uses, as you'll find out in this chapter. As an example, here is how you can reply to the question "What do you do?"

"You know how people nowadays are finding it harder to get ahead, what with corporate downsizing, the lack of job security and the higher cost of living?"

"Well, what I do is, help them set up their own business, so they can start taking care of themselves and their families once again."

"Let me ask you – what do you do?"

You see how this paints a picture of how what you do helps others? The very essence of Natural Selling®! Your reply focuses on some challenges that are in the world that most people are aware of and can easily identify with and, it demonstrates your purpose, which is to help other people solve these challenges. It is also a focused reply. It demands you understand what you do in the context of helping others.

Now if a person identifies with this, and is finding it harder to make ends meet, or if they're facing downsizing, do you think they are likely to want to know more? Most probably 'yes!' And do you want to tell them? Yes, of course you do. Do you want to do it now? You can if you want, but then what would you be doing . . . presenting what *you* think they should hear, because you don't have any reference point about them.

So my suggestion is wait. Find out more about them and who they are so that you can possibly customize your answer. That's why you ask the question, *"What do you do?"* at the end of your explanation. Asking a question like this is an invitation for them to participate in a conversation.

By stating how what you do helps others, you will have already created a good impression and you'll cement that by turning the conversation on to them. And remember, it's all in the questions. Contrary to the popular opinion that as long as you're talking, you're in control, the opposite is true. You actually control the conversation by letting go of your need to speak. Ask questions instead.

The Mechanics Of The Personal Introduction

Let me give you the mechanics for creating your own introduction. Comprised of three parts: problem, solution, question – here is how it works:

Problem

Start your reply with the phrase, "*You know how . . .*" and tag on to it the generic problems that your business opportunity can solve, problems that everyone can relate to. There are many problems and challenges in the world. Being a problem solver, your job is to discover them and find out what they mean to people. Problems such as:

> Job downsizing
>
> Lack of job security
>
> Higher cost of living
>
> High taxes
>
> Long travel time to work
>
> Low income
>
> Lack of free time
>
> Finding it harder to make and keep the money

Solution

Demonstrate how what you do helps people solve these problems. The key here is to use simple language, not clichés, or Network Marketing industry language such as residual income, time-freedom, time leveraging to name a few. These words have very little meaning to most people and can appear as if you're trying to sell something. You can start this part with, "*Well, what I do is help people,*" and then continue with:

> *"Start their own part-time businesses."*
>
> *"Get their lives back in control."*
>
> *"Have time to spend with their families."*
>
> *"Do the things they want to do."*
>
> *"Develop another income."*
>
> *"Replace their present job."*

Question

Ask a question to turn the focus back on the other person to start the process of exploring and uncovering whether they might have similar problems that need solving.

Keep it low key. The power of your response comes from using simple everyday language that everyone understands, without jumping out of the gate and hitting them with your solutions. We love what we do and can be so anxious to help and get the message out, we can think we have a hammer and everyone else is a nail! Use the above structure to build your own powerful response – use it and own it. It has many uses and you'll be gratified at the positive responses you'll get.

The Personal Introduction Is Flexible!

If you've already gathered a lot of information about someone, and they eventually ask you what *you* do, how do you think you can respond? By modifying your personal introduction to fit the things they are looking for. Let me demonstrate by assuming we have already spoken with someone and are replying:

"Actually it's interesting you should ask, because . . . ."

"You know how you were saying that having your child soon means you will need to give up your job, and it's causing you some concern because there will be a dip in your income and you're worried about being left behind in the business world?"

"Well, what I do is help people like you set up their own home-based businesses so that they can keep their business skills and, at the same time, make sure their family is being cared for."

"Maybe I could be of help to you?"

This speech has served me so well over the years; I can't imagine what I would do without it. It has many other uses, as you will discover in the rest of this chapter about the different ways of connecting with and starting effective conversations.

HOW TO START YOUR PRESENTATION
BY NOT PRESENTING

How do you think most people feel when they are expecting a presentation? Tense or excited to hear about all the wonderful things you are going to tell them? Do you find people move toward you or away from you when you present? Mostly people feel tense and move away. The fixed smile on the face and the greeting masks a fear.

Most people when being presented or 'sold' to, fear you are going to persuade them to do something. With this happening do you think you're going to get even one-tenth of their attention? Very unlikely! One of the worst errors a distributor can make is to present or propose solutions before discovering the deeper needs. People need to feel confident you have their best interests at heart.

So, when you're faced with making a presentation and you're tempted to tell someone all about the wonderful features and advantages of your products and business opportunity, my cautious advice is – don't, if you can possibly help it. Interview people instead!

You've already discovered that when you present, without having any knowledge of the other person, it's only your interpretation of what you think the other person needs to know. How many times have you made a presentation based on nothing more than your own guess and it ends with the other person saying, "I'll think about it" – or, "No, thank you!" And you're left feeling empty? Turn it around. Stop telling and start asking!

Even if someone says they would like to know more does not mean they will sit through a monologue of hearing what you have to offer.

ANSWERING THE HIDDEN QUESTION

Whether it's spoken out loud or not the hidden question from most people expecting a presentation is: "What have you got?" or "What do you want to tell me?" or "What do you want to sell me today?"

What's your first inclination, to tell them? Don't do it! Here is how you might want to respond. Whether you're asked a question or not, start by asking:

"Before I get into what I've got, let me ask you a few questions, so we can talk more about you and <u>what you're looking for</u>!"

For example, *"Tell me (more) about how your present job is going?"*

A statement followed by a question will immediately set the stage of gathering information for you. Use the answers you get to formulate your next questions, or use the questions in Stage 2 of the Conversation Framework.

Here are a few more starter phrases, for different situations:

"Before I get into what I've got, perhaps you would give me your thoughts on what we spoke about previously?"

"Before I get into what I've got, let me ask you a few questions to get an idea as to whether what I'm doing might fit into what you're looking for. If it does, great, if it doesn't, then maybe something else will work for you. For example, are you presently working?" or you can use another Background Question.

"Before I get into what I've got, it might be helpful to both of us, if I could understand a little more about you and what

you're looking for. For example, perhaps you could tell me more about the frustration you said you're having at work at the moment and how it's affecting you?"

You notice there is a common theme to starting the process, which is, *"Before I get into what I've got, or who I am, or what this is all about . . . tell me about you."*

It's downhill from there!

RESPONDING TO CALLS FROM YOUR ADVERTISEMENT

Some distributors I've spoken with complain that advertisements haven't worked. On closer examination, it appears their ads have worked because they got calls. What didn't work was the way they responded to the call. It appears they went into full gear presentation mode when the other person asked them what it was about!

Answer for yourself this question. Why are they calling? Because they are looking for something! All you need to do is ask and find out.

Interview Them!

Instead of attempting to convince your prospective customer by 'presenting' how wonderful you, your product, service and company is, 'interview' them. Find out what they're looking for to see whether your solution fits their needs! The point is – is it they interviewing you, or you interviewing them, when they call you? It's actually both – except *you* have the vehicle that could change someone's life, which is why they called you in the first place!

Here is an effective conversation starter that will start the process for you. Suppose someone calls you and asks: "I'm replying to your advertisement – could you tell me what it's about?" You would reply:

"I'd be delighted to! Before I get into what it's all about, let me ask you a question. What was it about the ad that attracted your attention?"

You will now have some 'signs' on the signpost as to why the person called. After they have answered, you ask another question:

"Was there anything else that attracted you?"

And you will have further signs. Now you have something to work with. You then continue asking questions based on his/her answers, or you use a background question you have ready, such as . . . *"Can I ask what you're presently doing?"* or *"Do you have an idea as to what you're looking for?"*

Asking them this last question is invaluable. You get a complete history of where they are and what they have done about their present situation. Remember, while the vehicle to get what they want is important, it's not half as important as to why they want to change.

Here is the three-step formula to do this:

Step 1: Ask what *attracted* them to the ad.

Step 2: Ask if there was anything else that attracted them. (Tell me more!)

Step 3: Ask them to expand on what they said, or ask Background Questions to start getting some facts.

By the way, if they ask you what it's all about, use your personal introduction if it's appropriate!

HOW TO CALL LEADS FROM A LEADS LIST

Let's establish that calling leads from a genuine lead list is not cold calling! (A cold call is calling someone you have never met and don't know about. It's like pulling a name randomly out of the phone book.)

Leads are like bananas; they ripen quickly, so use them promptly. If time is an issue think about handing some out to your associates. If you're reticent about calling the leads, remind yourself you're calling someone who has asked you to call. It's impolite not to return their request!

The leads you get from a bona fide lead list are from people who are looking for a change. So your job is to find out what that is and interview them. This is because it's your company and you want them to sell *you* on the idea they should join you, and stop trying to sell them! Now that's abundance thinking!

Why do you want them to sell you? Well, you have a potential solution for one, and secondly you are looking for the right people to work with you. If you were the VP of a big company and someone was looking for a job with you, would you attempt to sell them on joining you? Hardly likely! There's no difference. You are the CEO of your own company. So think and act like one. As Dale Carnegie said, ". . . happiness doesn't depend upon who you are or what you have; it depends solely upon what you think."

So here's the six-step formula for calling and connecting with someone from a lead list or even perhaps when you're returning their call:

<u>Step 1</u>: State who you are.

<u>Step 2</u>: Where you are from.

<u>Step 3</u>: Give them a 'heads up' as to why you're calling, by referencing and reminding them that they *asked* you to.

<u>Step 4</u>: Ask them if this is a good time.

<u>Step 5</u>: Discover if they are still looking.

<u>Step 6</u>: Find out their present situation and ask how you can help them.

Let's look at an example of this. Say I've chosen to return Mary's call:

<u>Step 1</u>: *"Hi Mary, this is Michael Oliver"*

<u>Step 2</u>: *"Of XYZ Company"*

<u>Step 3</u>: *"You recently enquired about a home-based business opportunity, and I'm calling to find out if I can help?"*

<u>Step 4</u>: *"Is this a good time for you?"*

<u>Step 5</u>: *"Good! Let me start by asking you a question – have you found what you wanted or are you still looking?"*

<u>Step 6</u>: *"Okay. Well, before I get into what I've got, perhaps you can tell me a little about you and what you're looking for, for example, are you presently working?"* (or ask some other Background Question.)

I've discovered the response to just one question can give you enough material to converse on for several minutes of meaningful relationship building conversation. People really do have the answers, all you need are the right questions – and to give them time to answer them.

Remember to:

- *Listen* to the answers.
- Ask questions to gather more information.
- Ask them to expand on their answers and where they are coming from.
- Ask them to expand on what they are looking for.

Following Up On Someone Who Has Been Sent Information

If you're following up on someone who has had information sent by someone else, like your company for instance, here is another 'opener.'

"Hi Mrs. Potential Customer, this is Michael Oliver from XYZ Company!"

"You recently asked us for some information regarding (Subject) and I'm following up on what was sent you! Is this a good time to talk?"

"Good! Can I ask you, what was it that interested you in getting the information from us?"

Notice you've already started your opening statement with a question! This ensures that the conversation stays on track. Constantly practice how to do that!

HOW TO SPEAK WITH FRIENDS AND PEOPLE YOU KNOW

Let's go over how you would open a conversation with your warm market. Before you do anything, prepare. It takes preparation, lots of preparation. It's 90% preparation and 10% execution – and I know from experience this is true for most people.

Here's a suggestion. When you put together your list of names, take the names you have and split them into two. One for friends and close acquaintances, and the other for people you know somewhat, such as people you do business with. I suggest you put the people you know somewhat into the category of 'How To Speak With Business Associates' that we will come to later. You can be a little more formal with them.

Now, create a separate page for each name. If you have a hundred names, create a hundred pages! Think about everything you know about each of those people. Write down everything you can about their family, their hobbies, their sports, their jobs, their relationships, and especially their likes, dislikes, passions, and so on.

Write down all the problems you might have heard your friends talk about, that your business opportunity might be able to solve – things like health problems or tight finances, and think, if you can, how it's affecting them. When you call, these are the things you are going to affirm, or find out. Spend time on this.

Then arrange the list from hot all the way to coldest. 'Cold' meaning someone you're least likely to connect with. Then start calling the coldest. Why do you do call the coldest first? Because you need to practice! You need to get your vocal chords and mind into gear. A great alternative to this is to do what someone I know does – he practices by talking to trees. And then he has the comfort of a backyard where no one can see him!

So, whenever you start the day with calls, my advice is always practice on your weakest contacts first, so you can get warmed up. However, think positively, think that the conversation will go well. Some of the coldest potential associates can turn out to be the most interesting and the most rewarding.

When you call, the three key things to remember are:

1. Respect the relationship that is already there. What's more important? Your friendship or your insisting you want them as a business partner?

2. Give the reasons why you're calling, such as to catch up, to reconnect, find how they are, etc.

3. Think about holding back from talking about your business opportunity. Wait until you have found out enough about their present circumstances. It might take several calls until you have established a real understanding of the circumstances that have created their Current Reality.

While you have your own agenda, which is to move your business along, the more important thing is to stay with your purpose to discover whether or not you can help them. Let your agenda guide your questions and not manipulate them.

When you start calling, focus your conversation on them and what is happening in their lives. If you haven't spoken for a long while, you can start off by saying something like:

"Hi Sandy, this is Michael. It's been quite a while since we last spoke and you crossed my mind the other day and I thought I would give you a call to catch up and see how you, Jeff and the kids are. Is this a good time to talk?"

You can then play 'catch up' and get some history of where your friends are in their lives at the moment. If you're calling someone you know quite well you might want to explore and expand on the challenges they might have mentioned in the past. Now you might be in a position to help. If they ask you what you're doing, you now know what to do – use your personal introduction!

Each conversation is going to be different, so vary your approach depending on the individual person. This is where your time spent planning pays off. You could open your conversations with phrases like:

"I was thinking about the challenge you were talking about the other day, and I was wondering how that was going."

"You know, I've been concerned about that health problem you've had for some while and I might have found something for you. But before I get into that – remind me about what is happening, then I will have a better idea as to whether it might be the right thing. For example . . ." and ask a question related to the subject.

"You know how you were talking about your lack of self-fulfillment at work the other day? Well, I might have found something that could be the answer for you! But let me ask you, how serious is the situation at work?"

Talk about work, relationships, health, and so on, and how the challenges in those areas are affecting them and perhaps their family. Do you think this is a familiar situation for a lot of people?

You might have two or three minutes, or you might have half an hour to have a conversation. The key thing here again is, don't rush this. This is about relationships and, for many of us, it's about re-establishing relationships from way back when, right up to the present. It's about understanding them, and probably very few of us really understand even our closest friends. So, get to know them.

Also, let me ask you this: Do you have to come to a conclusion in the first or even in subsequent conversations? Is it imperative you get your agenda, your business out on the table now? Only you know that! If you do not feel it's appropriate to bring up your agenda on this call, don't bring it up. The person you're calling is still going to be there next week or whenever.

I would suggest that carefully planting seeds is going to be far more powerful for you than hitting them over the head with the proverbial hammer. Seeds, if they are tended and watered, have the wonderful habit of turning into plants that bear a lot of fruit or flowers *if* you let them grow! Like plants, people bloom at different times. Your friends will be ready to seek your help at the appropriate time for them.

By taking this approach, you will, over a period of time, have planted so many seeds and understand so much more about your friends, that you will strengthen the relationship regardless of the outcome. A positive and mutually satisfying result of the process!

HOW TO START WARM CALLS USING
THE DIRECT APPROACH

There are probably some people you know who like more of a direct approach. This is for them. Ask your question around what you know about them; something they might be looking for.

- Introduce yourself and state the reason you're calling.

- Use and adapt your personal introduction.

- Ask a question.

This is how it could look:

"Hi Steve, this is Michael. I've come across something that might be of interest to you."

"You know how you were saying that you wish you could get out of your present situation because of all the politics going on at work and it was making you feel unfulfilled? Well, I've found something that might be what you're looking for."

"Do you have time to talk about it now with the idea we get together this week if it's of interest to you?"

ASK QUESTIONS AND QUALIFY BEFORE AN APPOINTMENT

Some people suggest going for the appointment as your first objective, and never divulge information beforehand. That can be a big time waster. Those are likely people who are insecure with their ability to communicate by phone. If someone isn't convinced to meet you, you want to find out now, rather than spending time and money going to an appointment that might or might not amount to anything.

Do Make A Confirmation Call

If you do set an appointment, call to confirm before you go. Some would say this gives them a chance to back out. Fine! If they do, they probably wouldn't have been there anyway when you did arrive. A phone call gives you a chance to address this and save time.

When you get together, continue your conversation by asking the relevant questions using the Conversation Framework as your guide.

SPEAKING WITH BUSINESS ASSOCIATES

Business people and people you know somewhat are also generally best approached in the more direct way. Put on the table the reason why you're calling, in a business like manner. They will respect you for that.

As you learned earlier, introduce yourself and the reason you're calling. Whenever you can, personalize the call, just as you do with your warm market and friends. Find a need or problem or something that might interest them if you can, and ask questions around that. For example:

"Hi Kathy, I'm calling you because I was thinking about what you said you were looking for the other week, and I've come across something that might be of interest to you. Would this be a good time to talk?"

"Hi Jill, you know how you were saying you were concerned about (describe what it is.) Well, I might have discovered something that could work for you . . . ."

"Joe, have you ever thought about being able to do something different from what you're doing now? Because I'm doing something to get me moving forward from where I am at the moment and would like to talk with you about it to see if it might be something you're looking for!"

If they ask what it is, you can reply with a customized version of your personal introduction followed by having a discussion based on asking further questions.

Plan your work and work your plan. Practice imaginary conversations with yourself. I do it all the time – having imaginary conversations with people – working out what I would ask, how they would reply and how I would respond to their answers. It's great fun because the conversations always work out the way I want them to. Interestingly enough so do most of the real 'live' connections. Magically, others feel the energy of quiet confidence as the right questions appear on the tip of my tongue.

How To Start Conversations With Strangers

'A stranger is a friend you haven't met yet.' And here is a simple way to start turning that stranger into a friend. Ask questions you normally use in your everyday life. Start off with Background Questions such as:

"What do you do for a living?"

"Where do you live?"

"Do you play any sports?"

"Do you have a family?"

Now, these questions are not random questions. There is a significant reason why you ask them. Each of these questions can start a process of uncovering and exploring potential problems or needs. You'll learn more about this in the next chapter. If a problem does surface in the course of your conversation, then you later link the specific problem to the specific features of your business opportunity that will solve the problem.

Let's look at a quick example: Say you ask someone in a supermarket line what he or she does for living. Later in the conversation it's revealed this person's main goal in life is wanting to create a community for disadvantaged children. You discover this cannot be achieved because they neither have the time nor the means to do it. What features of your business opportunity come to mind that you could propose to solve the problem? Part time (to build equity) or residual income perhaps? This is what I mean by linking problems to specific solutions.

When you take this conversational approach, it's amazing how quickly people will open up and reveal to you everything about him/herself. When the other person reveals their truth and you discuss it, you'll discover more ways to demonstrate how your solution makes sense to them than you'll ever imagine! You'll be bursting with ideas. However, if you jump right in with your solutions at this early stage, what's almost certain to happen? That's right, you will be forced into presentation mode, which puts the focus back on you. Stay calm. Continue to ask meaningful and relevant questions until you feel it's the right time to offer solutions.

WHERE STRANGERS MEET!

So, where *do* you meet these strangers? This question came up a while ago, when a friend of mine called me and asked me if I knew of any networking groups he could join. I asked him why, and he said he had exhausted the ones he knew about, and was seeing the same faces all the time.

I mentioned that I probably didn't know any more than he did, and suggested he do something. He has a house overlooking the city, so I said, "Walk over to your living-room window" which he did and said, "Okay, what am I looking for?" I said, "It's not what you're looking for, it's what you're looking *at*: A massive, fertile networking ground – the whole city in front of you!"

The point is, there are hundreds of places you can meet people. Let's talk about some of them:

How about the supermarket? Do you shop for food? Do you go to the supermarket, or the store once a week to save time? How about going five times a week? Do you go when it's the least busy or when it's the busiest? How about going when it's busiest? Do you get into the shortest lines or the longest lines? How about getting into the longest line you can find? Getting the picture? Be creative!

And, in these long lines, with whom are you going to talk to – the person in front of you or the person behind? The person behind! Why? Because you have a longer time to spend with them. Be creative! And, if the conversation isn't going anywhere – what do you do? You excuse yourself mumbling something about having forgotten the sugar, get the sugar, and join another line. Have fun with it. I know a lady who is very effective at doing this and shops every day in the local supermarkets.

What about banks? Do you go to the ATM machines to draw out money once a week? Again, draw your money out more often and go to the teller. Why? Because, you've got it – there's bound to be a line. Go when it's most busy, such as at lunch time. Get out there! There are millions of people just dying to tell you all about themselves.

And it's okay if you only have a couple of minutes. Just practicing starting conversations will boost your confidence and skills.

What To Say To Strangers

So what kind of conversation might you have in these lines? Well, use your imagination for how you can start one, whether it's about the weather, a magazine article on the racks, a compliment on what they're wearing, etc. And follow up with something like this:

"Are you from around here?"

"No, I'm just visiting!"

"Oh! Where are you from?"

"I live in Boulder, Colorado!"

Talk about this and, at an appropriate moment say,

"You know, maybe you can help me. Would you happen to know of anyone in your area who's been downsized or thinking about starting their own business, as I'm looking for someone in that part of the country to work with?"

If you're asked what kind of business you're in, use your personal introduction.

If they happen to respond they do know of someone, ask about them and get information on the other person. If they do live in the area, modify the question. And, if you're getting to the end of the line and feel you need to progress more with the conversation, then suggest you get together for coffee or tea or exchange names and phone numbers.

HOW TO START COLD CALLS

I'm always being asked, "How do you make cold calls?" This demonstrates to me an endless fascination for them. Cold calling can be a lot of fun, and might be the only way for you to connect with people if you live a great distance from a large population. They probably get you the most 'No's' of any other way I know, but they allow you to hone your questioning skills for nothing!

A key is to be relaxed, and not to sound as if you are reading from a canned script (which you're not as this is one of the reasons you're reading this book), and not to take the 'No's' you will get personally!

Cold calling is not calling from a bona fide lead list, or calling a referral, or calling back someone who expressed an interest in a home-based business. Cold calling is when you call someone at random from the telephone book or a company directory: Someone you've never spoken with before! That's cold calling! If you're good at it, it's very rewarding. It's all an attitude of mind and how you approach it!

There are five steps to cold calling and don't pause as you go through – just let it flow:

Step 1: Confirm you're talking with the right person.

Step 2: Give your name and the company you represent.

Step 3: Acknowledge their time.

Step 4: Give an interesting reason why you are calling, by using your personal introduction. Create interest and need by opening with a specific or generic problem most people can relate to.

Step 5: Ask a question by asking if there is interest. If there is, continue to ask questions to discover and explore. If there is not, bow out graciously!

Here is how it might look:

"Hello, is this Mr. Jones?"

"Mr. Jones, my name is Michael Oliver and I'm with a company called XYZ."

"I hope I've caught you at a good time . . . ."

"The reason I'm calling is, well, you know how people nowadays are finding it harder to make and keep the money they earn, what with lack of job security, corporate downsizing and high taxes?"

"Well, what I do is, help them set up their own full- or part-time home-based business, so they can start taking care of themselves and their families once again."

"Does this strike a chord with you, Mr. Jones? Does this seem like something that might be of interest to you?"

I think you'll agree this is somewhat different from most of the telemarketing calls you get in the evenings.

If they say, 'Yes,' continue asking questions. If they say, 'No,' either thank them for their time, or continue the conversation if you feel comfortable, by asking them if they know of anyone else who might be looking for something like this. If they refer someone to you, (or whenever you get a referral from anyone, come to that) here's how you handle referrals:

HOW TO CALL REFERRALS

When you get a referral, remember to do more than just thank the person who gave it you. This is the best time to ask the question: *"Tell me more about this person and why you think they might benefit from what I have?"* Doesn't it make sense to get as much of the background as you can about the referral? It will give you a picture and possibly several reference points to start a conversation. Here's an example:

"Hi Mary, I'm Michael Oliver and a mutual friend suggested I give you a call as I understand from her that you are having a challenge with . . . (you describe the challenge) and she thought I might be able to help. Is this a convenient time to talk?"

You then ask questions about their challenge. And, if they ask you what it's all about, you customize your personal introduction to fit what you understand they are looking for!

How To Continue An Earlier Conversation

A powerful way to continue a previous conversation is to pick up a relevant point that a person said to you. So you might say at your next meeting:

"You know, I was thinking about our conversation last night.. And you said something interesting . . . !"

"You said . . . ." (repeat what they said)

"Tell me more about that."

Have you noticed what you're doing here? You're demonstrating that you have listened to them – validating them or their point of view. And you're now asking them to expand on something to get a clearer understanding, to make sure you're in the same tunnel, and on the same track, so as to move whatever was formerly discussed forward. Make sure it is important *and* relevant to what you would like to explore.

'Continuing phrases' are also useful in other situations in which you might find yourself. You can also use this approach to restart any conversation. Have you ever found yourself reflecting on a previous conversation and wishing you had come up with the perfect answer? Or, if you're like me, have you come up with the perfect answer or question to ask about three hours after you needed it? I heard that Winston Churchill's famous 'one-liners' and speeches were mostly worked out, re-hearsed and stored for later use way before they tripped out of his mouth. It's like 'overnight' successes. 'Overnight' being a word for preparation over time! Well, you can always go back at a later time and start the conversation with:

"You know, I was thinking about our previous conversation . . . .and you asked /said . . . ." (repeat what they said)

"I believe I've found an answer to that!"

HOW TO START A 3-WAY CALL

3-Way Calling is an essential Network Marketing communications tool and any successful distributor will attest to its effectiveness. One of the secrets is to assume nothing about the person with whom you are going to talk.

We'll assume in this demonstration I'm the leader in this 3-way conversation, and I have been asked by you, my distributor, to talk with Mary. I have never met Mary, and I also know nothing about her, so I might ask:

"Hi Mary, I appreciate the opportunity to help you."

"Mary, just so I don't go over things you've discussed with my associate, would you give me your thoughts on what you've already spoken about, and what you would like to cover, so we can focus on you and what you're looking for."

Here is another example:

"It might be helpful to both of us if I could understand more about you and what you're looking for – do you mind if I ask you a few questions? For example, . . . ?"

LISTEN to the answers, and then ask your ongoing questions by simply relating your questions to the answers you've been given. You'll soon know what points to focus on to come to a mutually beneficial logical conclusion.

How To Connect With A Group

For small groups such as at an in-home demonstration, I suggest you steer away from presenting and allow the members in the group to interact with each other. I can remember getting a call from a distributor who was associated with a company that produced health products. She asked me for some advice on how to have a meeting with six friends who were coming over to her house. She felt uncomfortable doing the usual presentation with flipcharts, products, whiteboards, testimonials, overhead slides, etc., and wanted to do something more effective.

I asked her if the six people were aware of what they were meeting about, and she said, "Yes, they were." So I asked her what she thought about sticking all her gear into a closet somewhere, keeping it handy in case she needed it, and treating the meeting as a gathering with her acting as a facilitator and guide, asking questions about the group's issues over their work and the products they were presently using. I suggested she simply open the meeting declaring why they were together and ask them to share the challenges they had with their health, work and finances, and how it was affecting them, what they were doing about it and so on, before exploring her solutions.

The meeting was a success, with four out of the six either buying products and/or wanting to know more about the business opportunity. In the course of events only matters of relevance and meaning to the participants were discussed, and only products of interest were brought out. Everything else stayed – where? In the closet! This was a classic example of problem solving by focusing on people and their issues.

Now we can explore how to take the conversation starters further and understand how to use the most important part of the Conversation Framework – Stage 2 – The Discovering Stage.

CHAPTER 12

Stage 2: The Discovering Stage

*If you want to 'see' another person, listen to
their heart with your heart!*

The Discovering Stage is the heart of Natural Selling® and is the most important stage in The Discovery Process. If there is a partnership or 'sale' to be made – The Discovering Stage is where it's made because this is where the relationship is established! People psychologically 'buy' *you* first and will be open to listening to you based on your ability to demonstrate you can *listen, understand, respect and respond* to them and their unique needs.

The Discovering Stage combines questioning and listening skills. It does away with the traditional sales techniques of 'presenting,' 'objection handling,' 'telling your story,' and 'closing' when you first meet someone. You don't have to 'close' people when they are drawn to you during the *process* and are prepared to listen to the possibility you can help.

A clue to knowing you are making an impression is in the depth of the history the other person tells you. You are likely to hear things that have never been told to anyone else. Facts and feelings about their life will surface that have been buried deep in the past.

Using dialogue, and letting your personal objectives and agenda guide, not dominate you, you progressively travel through The Discovering Stage until you get to one of the three 'destination' points or logical conclusions of another person:

1. No Need.

2. Need. No desire to change.

3. Need. Desire to change.

Getting to one of these points is 'mapped' out for you by the answers you get. As you discovered in chapter 6, answers are like signs on a signpost springing up in front of you! You just follow the signs (answers) by asking more questions related to what you heard. As you do so, new signposts with new signs will pop up as you travel down the road together to one of the destinations. Taking advice from the words of Stephen Levine: "Buddha left a road map, Jesus left a road map, Krishna left a road map, Rand McNally left a road map. But you still have to travel the road yourself."

FASTER, LONGER, DEEPER RELATIONSHIPS!

Building a clear, complete, understanding of people in The Discovering Stage will help you make more commitments and achieve your own objectives faster and easier.

Whether it's on the phone or in person, The Discovering Stage is where you:

- Cement a new or strengthen an existing relationship.
- Get a precise picture of what your potential partner wants.
- Help your potential partner *think* about their needs and wants that will persuade him or her into thinking about making a change.
- Identify the emotional reasons – the 'why' behind what they are looking for by asking feeling questions – and putting some urgency into making a change.
- Determine if you can be of service by qualifying them to make sure they are serious about changing their present circumstances.

NO MORE REJECTION OR OBJECTIONS!

The process will eliminate objections and rejection if handled with good intent. If objections do come up, or you get rejected, it's probably because you've slipped back into those bad habits of presenting your solution or talking about yourself too early! Resist this! Move slowly for faster and longer lasting partners!

Don't Rush The Discovering Stage!

You are preparing and cementing the foundation on which the success of the ongoing relationship is going to be placed. If you don't have time to get it right the first time, when will you have time? If time is an issue, consider continuing your conversation later. Who said that every sales conversation has to have a final conclusion? Spend the time and people will spend the time listening to how you can help them! Later, these same feelings will carry over, as they become your partner. Don't rush the discovering. *Selling is the art of solving problems through patiently asking questions and listening.*

> *Selling is the art of solving problems through patiently asking questions and listening.*

The Process Never Differs – Only The Conversations!

The process is the same no matter with whom you're talking. You work from the same philosophy, using the four principles and methods that are manifested through dialogue. Your conversations are like normal ones you have at any time with anyone, except the difference now is that they are fuller, richer and more skilled.

The Discovering Stage is complete when you have fully qualified your prospective partner and are ready to move into transitioning into The Presentation Stage. (Or, bowing out if you discover you can't help.) Having said that, you will find yourself continually returning to the stage, to explore, understand and clarify new information as it comes to light. This can happen even after the 'sale' is consummated. The Discovering Stage is your 'bread and butter' of all the stages. As you master it, you will never use anything else again!

OVERVIEW OF THE FIVE DISCOVERING STAGE QUESTIONS

The following is a snapshot of the five types of questions used in The Discovering Stage and what they do. Each step will be explained in this chapter with a Conversation Guideline at the end, along with an example of an imaginary conversation.

The Discovering Stage Questions are developed from:

- Ones you learn in this book to start and continue conversations.
- Answers you get to your previous questions.
- Answers to questions you never asked.

The five questions are:

1. Background Questions
2. Needs Awareness/Development Questions
3. Consequence Questions
4. Solution Questions
5. Qualifying Questions

1. Background Questions

These get the facts about the other person's Present Situation:

"What is your present situation?" or, *"How did you get to this point in your life?"*

2. Needs Awareness/Development Questions.

Needs Awareness Questions uncover any potential problems or needs:

"Do you like your present situation?"

Needs Development Questions confirm the existence of a problem and explore the depth and the circumstances causing it. They open your potential partner's emotional doors by turning their *'objective facts'* into their *'subjective reality!'* The answers you get give both of you a clear picture of specifically *what* he/she wants or doesn't want, and *why* it's important to them. For example, "I want to have more time with my kids" (why?) "Because I'm feeling depressed about not being able to give them the care and attention they deserve."

"What do/don't you like about your present situation" and *"Why do/don't you like your present situation?"*

3. Consequence Questions

These explore the possible consequences or downside of leaving a problem unresolved, or not having the right solution. They can also uncover possible problems or needs that have not previously been thought of:

"What will you do if you don't do anything about your present situation?"

4. Solution Questions

These involve your potential partners in coming up with their own solutions. (They are fascinating questions as people tell *you* what the *explicit* benefits of solving their problems are!) They explore the upside consequences of having the right solutions:

"What would you do about your present situation?"

5. Qualifying Questions

Confirm that your potential partner is prepared to change their present circumstances. Qualifying Questions are used from the moment you start your conversation:

"Are you prepared to change your present situation if . . . ?"

These five categories of Discovering Stage Questions do not have to be asked in sequence. While it's possible to do so, conversation is not so linear. Move about this stage with freedom. Sometimes you'll get an answer to a question you never asked, so you don't need to ask it, though do have further material on which you can expand on or use later. Print a picture of the Conversation Framework firmly in your mind so you know where you are at any time in the conversation and know when to ask the right question.

Remember to clarify, feedback and summarize at every opportunity as you go. Keep moving forward until he/she has no more to tell you.

IMPLIED NEEDS TO EXPLICIT NEEDS

As you progress through The Discovering Stage, you'll likely hear what are known as 'Implied Needs.' Implied needs are statements about problems, challenges or concerns a person has. An example would be: "No, I'm not happy thinking about having to stay with this job for another eight years before I retire." This is a rather broad statement of need. If you offer your solution at this juncture, you are likely to meet rejection because it's too soon. While here is an implied indication or desire to change, this person needs to be more explicit about their need.

You can explore turning an implicit need into an explicit need by asking effective progressive questions until the explicit need is declared. Asking progressive questions is like playing pool. In pool the objective is to sink a ball *and* set the cue ball up to sink the rest of them. Asking questions has the same objective.

So if you followed the above statement with a Solution Question like this, *"How do you see yourself changing that?"* – you might get the reply, "If I could make some money doing something in my spare time that was flexible enough not to compromise my present job, I would jump at it!" Now is still not the time to present your business opportunity. There is a lot of information you've been given here, both said and unsaid, on which to find out more to get a better understanding. Asking questions like the following will further you in your quest:

"When you say 'more money' what do you mean by that?"

"Explain to me what you mean by 'flexible enough'?"

"I'm not sure I quite understand when you say, 'compromise your present job?' – perhaps you can expand on that."

Expand on the answers to the above questions as well, and soon you will have a complete picture of where this person is coming from, what they want, why they want it, and the degree to which they are committed to get it. Let the other person do the work for you. Let them tell you all the what's and why's. The more they say, the more they define to themselves why they need to change. Then you'll be able to comfortably offer a way you can help. *Understand to be understood.*

Understand to be understood.

Look at the five categories of Discovering Stage Questions in more detail.

1. BACKGROUND QUESTIONS

Background Questions create the foundation on which you build the rest of your conversation.

The previous chapter showed you how to begin any conversation putting the focus on the other person and starting the process of asking questions and gathering information. Background Questions are generally the next step where you get the *facts* about the present situation of the other person. You are asking:

- What is your present situation?
- Who are you?
- How did you get to this point?

While important, avoid asking more than three or four Background Questions in a row, as it can sound interrogative – as though you are reading a questionnaire off a list! They also tend to be logical and somewhat boring: There is little emotion in them, so you will get mostly logical and factual answers. So learn to expand the answers you get from asking a background question into **Needs Awareness/Needs Development Questions** as soon as you can. These are more interesting questions for people to answer. You'll notice the difference in the quality and quantity of the answers you get. Return to Background Questions as new information comes to light and as you need to broaden the foundation of your new knowledge! You will see how this works as you progress through this chapter.

F.O.R.M.S.

To help you form a questioning base, use the simple acronym: F.O.R.M.S. Family, Occupation, Recreation, Money, and Spiritual. It makes it easy to remember the subjects on which to base your questions. Remember to ask only relevant questions to start the process of uncovering potential problems.

'F' is for 'Family.' Ask someone if they have a family. Talk about the kids, vacations, their home, vehicles, college, etc. Here are a few questions to start off with:

"Are you married?

"Do you have a family?"

"How many are in your family?"

"Do your kids go to college?"

"Where do you live?"

"How long have you lived there?"

"Did you move from somewhere else?"

"Where were you before that?"

"What prompted you to move there?"

What's the importance of family? Well, if they mention they haven't had a vacation in a long time, or work long hours and don't get to spend time with the family, or that they don't know where the money will come from for college, or would like to live somewhere else, you have signs that 'money' or 'time' might be an issue.

This is also where the features of your business opportunity start popping into your head. Recollect that features are the elements of your business opportunity that solve the problem. So what features will start materializing here – 'Home-based business,' 'part-time work,' 'flexibility of work hours'? Don't jump to conclusions too early. The correct features will become clear as you progress more deeply into a conversation and discover the real issues. More information could come to light that could alter the first feature you thought of!

'O' is for 'Occupation.' Ask if they work, and if they do, get the facts about their job or business.

"Do you work for a living?"

"What kind of work do you do?"

"Where do you work?"

"How long have you been a . . . ?"

"What were you doing before that?"

"Do you travel to and from work?"

"Does that take you long?"

The answers you get give you choices as to what paths you want to take with further questions. Paths that could lead to hearing problems about downsizing, mergers, long-term viability of the job, lack of job security, lack of fulfillment. You might have the answer for them to get the financial security they could be looking for from the residual income feature, for example.

'R' is for 'Recreation.' Ask about vacations, hobbies, sports, golf, boating, bowling, etc.

"Do you have a hobby?"

"Do you play a sport?"

"What kind?"

"Do you like to travel?"

It could be that they have expensive hobbies, or have gifted children who play an expensive sport and don't have enough money to buy sports equipment. There could be expensive sports injuries that need attending to. Perhaps time is an issue. The list goes on . . . .

'M' is for 'Money.' Talk about the economy, social security and whether it affects them. Ask what they are doing to prepare for future retirement. Ask about investments. Ask what they do with their spare money each month. If someone complains about not having enough money or is concerned over their ability to retire some day, the 'part-time' or 'residual income' features are something to possibly discuss later in your presentation.

"Have you found the tighter job market affecting you at all?"

"Are you able to comfortably retire when you want to?"

'S' is for 'Spiritual.' Talk about the associations they belong to such as the Lions Club, or whether they attend church or a metaphysical association and what their beliefs are. They might have a deep-seated desire to be of more service to the world and don't currently have the resources or time to do so.

"Do you do any community or charitable work?"

Create a list of Background Questions. Start your questions around possible problems people have. Gather as much information as you can. Don't forget to move to Needs Awareness/Development Questions as soon as you can.

2. NEEDS AWARENESS/DEVELOPMENT QUESTIONS

These questions turn people's *objective facts* into *subjective reality* (their own interpretation of how they look at their life). They are developed from the information you gather from Background Questions or from answers freely given you. They expand on the facts and get behind them to explore and reveal feelings and emotions.

Remember, a decision to change is motivated by feelings. *When you hear the facts and are in no hurry to convert them into solutions, and instead focus on talking about the impact or the feelings that these facts might have on your prospective partner – people become drawn to you.*

NEEDS AWARENESS QUESTIONS

Needs Awareness Questions *start* the process of discovering someone's Current Reality bringing it into the present moment! Remember not to let your own reality re-interpret what they say to you. This is their conversation. Ask them to clarify and expand on what they say. And listen!

If you reflect on some of the work-related Background Questions that were covered, you'll see how the questions below follow on naturally. You could ask a Needs Awareness question like:

"So, what drew you into this type of work?"

To which you might get a reply, "I've always enjoyed organizing things and helping people." Two more 'signs' to decide in which direction to take the conversation – "organizing things and helping people." The answer is subjective. It's the perception of one person. Someone else is likely to give you a different reply. That's why it's so interesting to take this approach, because each conversation is different and yet the concepts and communication methods are the same. In this case, ask questions around the answer, "Organizing things and helping people." For, after all, aren't these two qualities ones you would like to hear more about? So open up the conversation and move towards finding further facts about this and the subjective reasoning behind the facts.

"What sort of things do you like organizing?"

And later you can ask:

"When you say 'helping people' – what does that mean to you?"

"What is it about your work that gives you that?"

You continue asking for more information until you can ask the basic question:

"Do you enjoy your work?" (Your present situation)

The answer will be a 'yes,' 'no,' or somewhere in between. Whatever it is, this is where you move to an important Needs Development Question. Before you do that, there is something important to consider.

TESTING THE TWO TRUTHS

Many distributors feel dejected if a person declares they love what they are doing, because they're hoping for the opposite response! But it doesn't matter whether they say 'yes' or 'no!' It doesn't matter whether they say they love their job or hate it. *It is what it is*, and you can't hope that they will say something you want them to say.

A reason it doesn't matter is that if you're patient, you'll discover that most people usually have *two truths*. Very few people love or hate 100% of what they do or where they are. There is always something that can be improved. You will be surprised by the amount of times you will hear people express their undivided attachment to something and later curse the day they ever got involved with it.

So, if a person says they do like what they are doing, the way for you to find out the predominant truth is to first ask *what they like* about their situation and then *what they would change if they could*. In many cases, you will find people contradicting what they had previously said. Sometimes the first answer will reflect their 'protected history' and the other tells you what they would really like to happen.

Demonstrate this for yourself with this exercise. Ask someone four questions: (1) where they live, (2) how long they've lived there, (3) if they enjoy living there (Most people in my experience will say 'yes'), (4) why they enjoy living there. Now ask the question, *"Where would you live if you could live anywhere in the world?"* It's almost certain the answer will be other than where they are presently living. Two truths!

Let's go back to the former conversation and let's say the person we're talking with answers that they enjoy their work. But on probing deeper, you could discover that the job only pays enough to get by and, given the chance, they would prefer to have both the enjoyment and the income. Or, it could turn out that time might be an issue. Ask and explore.

Here's an example. Some people love their job and the $150,000 a year they are making and yet hate the pressure and lack of fulfillment in their work – two truths that could be turned into one. Money isn't always everything. Money *and* fulfillment could be. It could also be that your business opportunity can offer both. The chapter on Current Reality explains why this is!

NEEDS DEVELOPMENT QUESTIONS:

Needs Development Questions finds this out for both of you. They help both of you to explore the reality of the present situation. Their answers paint a clear picture of *specifically what* they want or don't want and, more importantly, *why* it's important and how they feel about it.

So, whether a person answers in the affirmative or negative, follow the response you're given. If it's in the positive, go with it. Ask them everything they like about it. And don't short-change yourself here. It's important to know the things they like as well as the things they don't like. You need to make sure your solution can continue giving them the enjoyment they currently have.

Conversely, if the conversation starts up the path of 'don't like,' expand on that. Later, explore what they 'do like.' Get the balance – be interested in all sides of the equation. The predominant truth will surface!

Needs Development Questions is the one place in The Discovering Stage that you would be well served to pay a lot of attention to. They:

- Encourage people to expand on their opinions, feelings, emotions, worries, likes and satisfactions, dislikes and dissatisfactions, and how it's affecting them.

- Give both of you a clear picture of specifically what the problems are (if any) and why the need to change is important.

- Make you look very professional and let people consider you as an insider – not an intruder. You form a bond other distributors can only fantasize about. While they only get the facts, *you get the facts and the feelings!*

TWO PATHS OF QUESTIONING TO FOLLOW

The following questions will assist you in finding the predominant truth. Remember: Be conversational and put these questions in your own words if you wish. Use them as a base to build further questions around the answers you get. Practice them by having imaginary conversations with yourself, or practicing with associates.

I've given you the way to explore both paths no matter whether the other person answers 'yes' or 'no' to the question, *"Do you like what you do/Where you live/What you have/etc.?"*

As your conversation progresses and you broaden your understanding, other paths will develop. Conversation is like a rising river: It will develop its own tributaries. This is what you want. More tributaries mean more opportunities to explore and deepen the relationship. Relax and remember the main points you hear on which to ask for more. The more you relax, the more you remember.

Make sure that whatever path you walk first, walk up the other one! Otherwise you won't know what's there! Heed the words of the poet Antonio Machado, "Travelers, there is no path. Paths are made by walking." Each new piece of information that is presented to you is a new path. Discover what's up them with these Needs Development Questions!

PATH 1

Using work as an example and in response to the answer, "Yes, I love my work . . ." here is a sequence of questions you can ask to explore more deeply what they mean and whether they mean what they say:

"What do you like about your work?"

"Why do you like (What you just told me)?"

"Is there anything else you like about your work?"

"Why do you like (What you just told me)?"

"Why is doing all of that important to you?"

"How does it make you feel doing that?"

<u>*"What would you change about your job if you could?"*</u>

"Why would you change . . . ?"

"Why is that important to you?" ("What would that do for you?")

"How do you feel about that?"

"Is there anything else you don't care about . . . and would change?

"How does that make you feel not to have what you just said you wanted?"

PATH 2

In response to the answer, "No I don't like (my work . . . .)" Here is a similar sequence of questions you can ask:

"What don't you like about your work?"

"Why don't you like . . . (What you just told me)?"

"Is there anything else you don't like about your work?"

"Why don't you like . . ." (What you just told me)?

"Why is that important to you?"

"How do you feel about that?"

<u>*"What do you like about your work?"*</u>

"Why is that important to you?" ("What would that do for you?")

"How do you feel about that?"

"Is there anything else you do like about your work?

"How does that make you feel having that?"

Remember you can rephrase all these questions to suit your own style and personality. For example, you could rephrase, *"What would you change about your job if you could?"* to, *"Is there anything you would change about what you're doing if you could?"*

You might not use all the questions. Use what is appropriate moving between facts and feelings. You can't intellectualize this process. You have to do it to experience it. It's like learning a foreign language. What would be more effective? Learning a new language from a book or going to the country and immersing yourself in it? Observe yourself doing it as well as being the participant. Feel the power of having conversations like this.

Many answers can come from one question. Explore the answers to broaden your base of understanding of the circumstances that have brought a person to the present moment. Talk about the answers you get, and 'slip' the questions in.

Don't interrogate by rattling the questions off like a machine gun.

The more time you can spend in the developmental stage, of bringing the other person into the present moment, the greater your success rate will be. You will hear a lot of information that might seduce you to bring up your solution too early. Hold back. Broaden the map. *Go for the heart – not the throat!*

ONE TRUTH WILL DOMINATE

Having traveled the two paths, if you discover that the dominant truth is one of unhappiness with the present circumstances and you have sufficiently understood the reasons, you can start exploring the future – the dream unrealized – the dream that could be realized. As you ask about the future it will now have the present situation to be compared against. Perhaps they will come to the conclusion that their current reality is no longer an option. Perhaps they will be thinking it's now time to move forward and grow. If you feel this is the case, the question to ask to find out is:

"What would you rather be doing if you could?"

Ask them to tell you more, and then interject:

"How would that make you feel if you could do that?"

As Peter Senge states, "It's not so much what the vision is – it's what the vision does.'

Continue talking about what you heard, finding out more, allowing the other person to expand and listen to their future vision. Strengthen your own understanding of the process further.

Let's look at understanding and strengthening some more communication skills before moving on:

- Deeper Feeling Finding Questions
- Clarifying And Expanding
- Tell Me More – Tell Me More – Tell Me More

Deeper Feeling Finding Questions

"How do you feel about that?"

You know now you can create a relationship by understanding more of the essence of a person by finding how they *feel* about their present circumstances, and how they *would feel* if those circumstance could be changed. In doing so, you also allow them to influence themselves into making a change. One of the most significant feeling questions you can ask is, *"How do you feel about that?"*

I can remember asking this of my father who was taking a large number of pharmaceutical drugs after an operation for a condition he had. There was a problem with them. The side effects were disabling him by making him drowsy and slowing him down. As they were what the doctor 'ordered,' he had a faith in that they were the right thing to take as he is respectful of the medical profession.

Being concerned about him, and a great believer in nutritional products for prevention and cure, I suggested the idea that he explore how he could take more natural remedies, which might address the cause of his condition and eliminate the side effects. Initially he wasn't open to it and it was frustrating to know that a natural remedy was at hand that could reduce or eliminate the side effects of his prescribed drugs. I knew pressuring him would close him down to ever being open, so I didn't! I just asked simple questions whenever I called to keep my finger on the pulse without hounding him.

The turning point came at a later date when he was talking about the continuing frustration of being unable to do things he used to. I asked him with all the care in my heart, *"And how do you feel about that?"* There was the longest pause and eventually a very tired and dejected voice replied, "I feel like an old man!"

At this point we were able to talk about alternative approaches and do the necessary research to replace some of the drugs. Time and the inability to lead a normal life had made the discomfort more noticeable. He was preventing himself from 'being himself.' By talking about it and hearing his own words he realized it was time to look for alternative remedies. And he did!

Do the same thing yourself. Be interested in everyone you meet. Keep your own ideas and thoughts to a minimum. Don't put words in people's mouths by suggesting things based on your own reality! Continually clarify and expand on what is said. Learn the people skills necessary for you to make a difference. You get what you give. In the words sung by four famous poets, 'The love you take is equal to the love you make.'

CLARIFYING AND EXPANDING

In addition to the powerful question, *"How do you feel about that?"*, consider using these types of phrases as well, whenever appropriate:

"Can I ask why you want that?"

"Can I ask why you said that?"

"What does that mean to you?"

"Have you ever thought about . . . ?"

TELL ME MORE – TELL ME MORE – TELL ME MORE

The answer to a first question on a new subject is usually an answer that can actually mask the real answer. If you accept it 'as is' you are likely to miss it. The first answer can also be relatively superficial or even something that is made up. It's like the outer layer of the onion. Peel off the layers and see what's behind each one until you get to the essence of where the other person is coming from. Listen for it. Ask your potential partner to expand on their answers. The rewards are immeasurable.

Reflect on the three rules of buying real estate: Location, location, location! It's the same with Natural Selling®: Tell me more – Tell me more – Tell me more! Here are some questions you can use to help you do that.

"Tell me more about . . .?"

"Would you elaborate on . . .?"

"How does your spouse/partner feel about that?"

"Could you expand on that?"

"Why do you still feel that way?

"What do you mean when you say . . .?"

"Is there anything else I should know about . . .?"

"Did I understand you to say . . .?"

"Why do you say that?"

"So what you're saying is . . .?"

You learned about some of these questions in chapter 7 and chapter 8: 'How To Listen' and 'What to Listen For.' You might want to revisit these chapters to refresh yourself.

3. Consequence Questions

These explore the possible consequences or downside effects of a person's present situation and tend to make people go inward and think more about their decision, or even lack of decision, to change or not to change it. Consequence Questions revolve around asking the basic question, *"What if . . . ?"*

"What if you didn't do anything and the situation got worse?"

"What if the course of action you're thinking of taking didn't get the answers you're seeking?"

To formulate them, take a problem and ask a question that reveals and explores the possible consequences of:

- A problem that the other person is not aware of
- Leaving the present situation unresolved.

A PROBLEM THAT THE OTHER PERSON IS NOT AWARE OF

Sometimes your knowledge can see things that others don't. Let's say your potential partner felt that changing their company would be an answer to the challenges they have with the present one. Your knowledge might tell you that all that's likely to change is the color of the wall and the carpets, especially if they are looking for the inner actualization that few companies can give them. So, instead of telling this directly, you could help them consider the ramifications of their decision by asking: *"What if nothing changed by going to another company?"* or, *"Have you considered how you would feel if changing to another company didn't get you the personal results you said you were looking for?"*

Let them answer and reflect on their decision to open up the conversation that will eventually allow you to talk about what you know. If they can't see any ramifications, you can suggest what they might be, by saying, *"My experience has shown me that all that changes in most cases is the color of the carpets, have you ever considered that?"*

LEAVING THE PRESENT SITUATION UNRESOLVED.

There are people who like to procrastinate. Put some urgency into them by reflecting on what they said earlier and asking something like:

"Have you thought about how it will affect your ability to take care of your family if you let things go on as they are?"

"Have you considered what you would you lose by waiting until you retire?"

Here are some more opening Consequence Question phrases you can use to help you surface the implications of taking or not taking a course of action. These starter phrases have the capacity to develop the potential problems behind the problems:

"What will happen if . . . ?"

"What if it didn't work out?"

"Would that concern you if . . . ?"

"What would it mean to you if you weren't able to get what you're seeking?"

"Do you see any problems with not having everything you want fulfilled?"

"How would that affect your ability to get the self fulfillment you said you were seeking?"

"What would it mean to you if you couldn't . . . ?"

"Would it worry you if you didn't get . . . ?"

"How would you feel if you weren't able to . . . ?"

"How would that change . . . ?"

"What if you lost . . . ?

"Does that concern you?"

"What will you do if you cannot . . . ?"

"Have you thought about the consequences of . . . ?"

4. SOLUTION QUESTIONS

The opposite of Consequence Questions, Solution Questions explore the upside results of solving problems. These are very productive questions to ask because when you ask: *"What have you done about changing your present situation?"* or, *"What would you do . . . ?"* People tell you! *People have the answers, and their ideas form part of the solution!*

> *People have the answers, and their ideas form part of the solution!*

Research shows that the reason why top sales performers in the professional world of selling are so successful is that they ask many times more Solution Questions than average performers!

There are five reasons why Solution Questions are so productive:

1. You get a good picture of how people think, and what they are prepared to do.

2. People tell *you* (and, therefore, themselves) what *they see* as the explicit advantages and benefits of solving their problems.

3. *Their* ideas become part of the solution because it's not so much what they will physically do, or have done – it's how the change will make them feel.

4. They attach their feelings to the desired outcome.

5. You become associated with the good feelings that come from talking about the answers.

The answers you get to *Solution Questions give people a feeling of what it would be like to make a change and move forward*. Their answers lift their heads and their minds out of the mist to see the horizon of their dream again. They consciously and subconsciously see how taking action will turn their problems around. They *feel* the positive effects of having their present situation reversed through listening to their words. Usually the deeper the discomfort of the present situation, the more positive effect their answers will have on them.

Solution Questions have another advantage for you. They put a brake on your need to tell and come up with your solution too fast.

SOLUTION QUESTIONS MAKE YOU SHINE!

Few salespeople or distributors use this remarkable skill because first, not many people know about it and, second, they are afraid the answers they get won't be the ones they want. Why is this? Well, it's because they are afraid the other person is going to say something they don't want to hear, such as, "I'm going to change my company, my profession, or go back to school!"

However, you know differently. You know that people who want to change are usually looking for something that goes beyond just the logical mechanics of say, switching to another job. It's not so much as to what they will do, but what they want and *why* they want it, such as a sense of fulfillment, recognition, self-esteem, personal freedom, and so on. And the question is, are they likely to get it by doing nothing or changing their company? They might! But you know

Your enthusiasm for telling what you know can keep you from discovering what the other person knows!

they will if they join you, as they will be in a nurturing environment that can fulfill both their logical and personal requirements.

Distributors taking the more traditional approach also tend to feel that because they have the knowledge and the solutions, they must demonstrate them and come up with their solutions quickly to make it appear as though they are smart. *Their enthusiasm for telling what they know can keep them from discovering what the other person knows!*

Don't let your knowledge and your need to tell get in your way! Let the other person give you the answers to what they would do! You'll get the credit for it anyway. Why? – Because you were the catalyst. You listened and you became associated with the result. *Use your knowledge to ask questions, not to tell people what you know!*

Solution Questions can be asked anywhere at any time, even after you have made your presentation. They come in different forms depending on the context and the situation. So the two basic questions you can ask are:

1. *"What Have You Done About It, If Anything?"*

2. *"What Would You Do About It If You Could?"*

1. "What Have You Done About It, If Anything?"

Many people actively look for ways to change their present situation and explore different avenues. The way to find out whether they have done anything is to ask these types of questions:

"What have you done about it, if anything?"

"Have you looked for anything that would give you what you're looking for?"

If they have, you talk and ask them to expand on what they tell you. People who have attempted ventures are probably people you want to spend extra time with. You might also want to consider qualifying them extra hard to make sure they aren't the type that move to other venues as soon as the first hurdle comes along!

Whatever they have done, find out why they got involved with a particular venture, *what worked, what didn't work, what would they have changed and what criteria they would use to make a decision to do something else.* Use all your Discovering Stage Questions to get a picture of each thing they did. You will see trends in the answers and then you can offer them the opportunity of working toward what they want.

Let's say a person is in the wilderness again after leaving their last Network Marketing Company because of the lack of training. Perhaps the experience left them looking not too kindly on the industry. Instead of defending the industry, which is a normal response, with, *"Yes, but we're not like that – and we can give you all the training you want"* answers – ask them what happened.

It doesn't matter whether what they say to you is true or not. To them it was. It doesn't matter that they might have failed because of the limitations of their own beliefs. At least they have tried and you can help them challenge their perception of their experience by asking Discovering Stage Questions until you come to a point where you can ask the question:

"Appreciating what you've gone through, what if the industry isn't what you think it is. What if your experience was an unfortunate incident, and what if you could get the right training so that you can get what you want out of life? Would you consider looking at it again?"

If you have built a good solid relationship to this point, the chances are strong they will. They got involved originally for a reason and I doubt that the reason will have changed much. I've met people who have been involved with two or three Network Marketing Companies that haven't worked out for them, and I always ask them the question:

"So what attracted you to the industry in the first place and why do you keep returning to it?"

The question reminds them of the many advantages that Network Marketing offers over any other type of industry or work. It also reminds them that perhaps all they need is to work with the right person. And who is the right person at this point in time? You are!

2. *"What Would You Do About It If You Could?"*

Most people have dreams or had a dream at one time. Things they did or said in their earlier life would have revealed this. Most people's dreams get buried in the big machine of life. People become institutionalized. In the words of Don Miguel Ruiz, in his book, *The Mastery of Love*, they become 'domesticated.' They exchange certainty for their dreams and freedom. They learn to become professionals, or claw their way to middle management as one clever TV ad put it. And when they get there, they get the money, car, prestige and a title. But none of this is the person. A title does not say who a person is – *who people are is what's inside of them*. Many have lost touch with this – their true, inner self, but often start seeking it again as they progress through life. The institutional world is a fertile ground for allowing people to lose their soul.

If you ask people:

"What would you do if you could do anything of meaning to you, and there was nothing to stop you?" And you give them time to think (and you don't let your need to feed them a bunch of examples before allowing them to reply get in the way), they will eventually give you an answer that usually goes deeper than just 'wanting to travel or play golf!' You know the answer is more likely to be one of wanting a sense of personal worth through contribution to the world and in the workplace.

A *Fortune* magazine survey in 1996 found that out of eight out of ten people would not stop working, even if they suddenly became wealthy enough not to do so. It was discovered that people are looking *to be of service by helping others.*

So ask Solution Questions and give time for people to think. Doing so allows them to get in touch with their soul. When they do, continue asking and connect your soul with theirs. Keep your focus on your intent to help. Some people have been stuck in their history for a long time: Stuck within the limits of what they don't know: Stuck within the limits of their geographical surroundings: Stuck within the limits of their own minds. Such limits are powerful everyday sedatives that have prevented them from moving forward to get what they want. Until you come along!

PROBE DEEPER

Ask people to expand on what they say in response to your Solution Questions and let them reveal the explicit advantages and benefits of what the solution will *mean to them* and *allow them to do.* Instead of accepting at face value what someone says, probe deeper and ask: *"Why is that?" "Why is that important to you?"* (This question is another way of asking, *"How do you see the benefits of solving your problem?"*)

The magic to the answers you get here is that your potential partner will sell himself or herself on the idea of change!

CONVERSATION EXAMPLE

Let's see how this works. Suppose you were having a conversation with someone who was complaining how the large premiums they were paying for their disability insurance was preventing them from doing the things they wanted, and you asked the Solution Question:

"What do you see as the answer to your problem?"

And the reply was, "To find some way to make more money to get my disability insurance payments taken care of." And you asked:

"Why is that?"

They might reply: "Because the payments are not allowing me to keep up with my friends wherever they go."

"Is that important to you?"

"Well, it's making me feel lost and saddened because we're drifting apart and we used to be really close."

You notice in this conversation, feelings come into the picture. It's full of feelings and if you ask these types of questions with care and compassion you will hear, see and feel them. And who else is hearing and feeling it? They are! Their Current Reality is now in the present moment and for many there will be a feeling of needing to change, and soon. And if you can help solve this last part of the conversation, you will be satisfying the personal needs by offering a benefit.

You might have noticed that this particular line of questioning was bringing out a feature that would possible solve this dilemma – residual income. If you think about it, the questions are revolving around the feature so that you can determine whether this might be the main one to talk about. Residual income could eventually take care of not having to make the payments thereby giving the person the opportunity to keep up with his/her friends whether in sickness or in health.

In this example, the person is telling you what they are looking for *and* the benefits of having the means to take care of their disability payments. All you have to do later is feedback what they said and talk about the feature of residual income to demonstrate how they can do it. On the other hand, if you bring up the solution yourself, especially early in the conversation, then you're likely to have to justify its usefulness.

So don't stop here. Find out more. Involve your potential partner. Let them challenge themselves! Ask the question:

"What's preventing you from making a change or doing it right now?"

Another way to phrase this is:

"What's stopping you from getting what you want?"

At this point the conversation could go into one of reflection. There might be signs of discomfort because the Current Reality and the Present Moment have converged. Additional information will come to light. The reply could be as simple as something as, "I've never found the right thing," whereupon you help them stay in the moment and consider asking a Qualifying Question like:

"What if the right thing came along – are you ever open to things like that?"

If we continue with our 'disability conversation' we could ask another Qualifying Question:

"So if you could find a way of eliminating your disability insurance payments and yet always be covered, what would that mean to you?"

To which the response is almost guaranteed to be, "Well, that would be wonderful, how would that be possible?"

ADDITIONAL SOLUTION PHRASES TO USE

Here are some more examples of how to ask these questions. (These, of course, would be in response to conversations around specific topics.)

"John, you said you would love to be able to work more effectively; what would that do for you?"

"Suppose you could put in some of your time that would create an income that would be ongoing whether you were disabled or not – how would that help you?"

"Mary, if you could do something that could replace your present job over the next three to four years, what would that mean to you?"

"Is there any other way you can see how this would help you?"

"Why do you think it would be a good time to . . . ?"

"How would the rest of your family feel about you eventually achieving your dreams as well as bringing home the income?"

Now you have a good picture of where a person is coming from, what they want, why they want it, etc., it's time to see if they are really interested in changing their present circumstances by asking them a Qualifying Question before moving through The Transitioning Stage to get to The Presenting Stage.

5. QUALIFYING QUESTIONS

A lot of people want things they can't have or won't work for. So, qualify them before you give them all your serious attention. The main purpose of qualifying is to make sure you don't waste your time and someone else's if they are not ready to make a change. Qualify! Qualify! Qualify! Qualify at the beginning of your conversation, during your conversation, and just before you present your opportunity.

The Discovering Stage in Natural Selling® is in itself a process of continual qualification no matter what the 'Questions Title' might be. Most of the questions you ask are subliminal qualifying steps along the journey of discovery. Sometimes the answers you get back will make it obvious there is a strong commitment to change. You won't have to qualify as firmly because the desire to change has already been stated in what is said and in the way it's said.

Qualifying commits people! For example, you could frame a Solution Question like this:

"So would you tell me how you see working for yourself would change things for you?"

Letting the other person reply in their own words, they psychologically qualify and commit themselves. This is for their benefit as much as yours!

Qualifying helps people reflect on making the next step to change. Again, it comes from hearing their own words as they speak to you.

Qualifying and asking for approval or clarity allows you to eliminate any misunderstandings or misinterpretations. At the same time, the other person reinforces and anchors their decisions as you progress through the conversation.

So:

- Qualify Before You Explore
- Qualify During Your Conversation
- Qualify Before You Present

QUALIFY BEFORE YOU EXPLORE.

More time is wasted by not qualifying people than anything else in selling, whether you're making a new call or following up on a lead. Before you start your 'sales interview' you need to hear an expression of interest and ability. You are looking for both an interest in changing and the ability to obtain the resources to start the process.

For example, if you are following up on a lead, you might ask:

"If you were fortunate enough to find the right opportunity that will get you what you want, can I ask if you're ready to make that change and if you are, do you have the financial resources to do it?"

This is your right to do so and switches the focus of you having to sell them, to them having to sell you. The experience is exhilarating.

QUALIFY DURING YOUR CONVERSATION.

Throughout your conversation, no matter where you are, use phrases like:

"How important is that to you?"

"Why is that important to you?"

"Is it important for you to solve the problem?"

"Why would you find that so useful?"

"I sense you're not too sure, how do you see it?"

"If you could . . . what would that mean to you?"

"How would you feel if you could . . . ?"

QUALIFY BEFORE YOU PRESENT.

At the end of the Discovering Stage, when you get to the point where you want to suggest your solution, the basic question is:

"Are you prepared to change your present situation to get what you want?"

It's like saying:

"Seems you have a problem! I might know of a solution! Would you like to know more?"

The classic close in traditional selling is, "If I could show you how to do that, would you be interested?" It's a good question but turns the focus back on to you. This can raise your tension level as well as the other person's. You will have gone right back into selling mode. Using the word 'I' can destroy rapport.

Rephrase and replace the above question with a qualifier like this:

"If there were a way you could get what you want . . . do you keep your eyes open for opportunities like that?"

Offering it like this removes the pressure. It excludes you, the 'distributor,' when you say it. By excluding you, you allow yourself to be *included* when you come to offer your solution later. Harmony and balance is maintained by the rules of dialogue. Using an analogy from the Wild West Days in the U.S., it's like checking your gun in at the door! Everyone is on equal ground. Actually, when you come to think of it, the whole conversation and ongoing relationship is like this.

As an exercise, say both the classical and the rephrased question out loud. Feel the difference and energy in each of them. See which one is more relaxed, conversational and comfortable for you!

There are two steps to qualifying before presenting:

1. Briefly Summarize
2. Qualify with a Question

BRIEFLY SUMMARIZE

Take the information you have heard and make sure you have it right by asking, for example:

"So, if I heard you correctly, you're looking for something that will give you <u>peace of mind and the recognition</u> for your efforts, is that right?"

When they say 'yes,' you qualify with a question.

QUALIFY WITH A QUESTION

"Let me ask you, if you could do something else and get all the things you said you wanted, so that you could feel you were moving your life forward . . . ? Would you make a change if an opportunity like that came along?"

You're almost guaranteed to get a 'yes' each time. Why? Because the question is based on what you were told the person wanted. If a person has spent some time telling you what is wrong with their present situation, and that they would change it if they could, how could they answer any other way? The degree of enthusiasm in the 'yes' might range from being guarded, such as, "Yes, depending on what it is." (Some people are naturally cautious) to, "Absolutely! Why, do you know of something?" (Don't expect a resounding 'Yes' if you've rushed the conversation.)

Here are a few more 'end of the phrase' Qualifying Questions you can use:

"Is that what you're looking for?"

"Does that look about right to you?"

"Does that work for you?"

"How do you feel about that?"

"Are you okay with that?"

"Would you agree with that?"

Here are some customized examples of how to use qualifiers. These would be in response to specific conversations. Adapt them for your own use:

"If you were ever presented with the opportunity to do just that – <u>would you do whatever it takes to get you the things you want</u>?"

"Mike, Let me ask you, it sounds as if you're frustrated with your present company, right? So, if you could get what you

said earlier that you wanted, <u>how important is it for you to do that</u>?"

"Mark, you told me you're going crazy in your job because of the uncertainty, the politics and lack of promotion for your work. If you could change all of that and do something different, <u>would you do it</u>?"

"Wendy, what if you found a way for you to realize your dream, <u>would you seriously look at making it happen if something came your way that gave you the opportunity</u>?"

"Sue, you told me that the criteria for working with a company is that it had good consumable products that were ethical and natural. If you found the right company with the right mix, <u>would you seriously make the move</u>?"

SUMMARY

Commit to memory all the above phrases and format. It's a framework within a framework and, like Kipling's *Six Wise Serving Men*, these questions will more than serve you well. Practice with an associate with the questions in front of you. Be comfortable with them. Feel how effective they are! Get them perfectly rehearsed so that the right words will come to you when you need them. You might not necessarily use the words you learned, but the right words you *need* will trip off your tongue! You don't need scripts when you're working from another person's wellspring of knowledge and answers that give *you* the next questions to ask.

When you get the positive responses you're expecting, then you move to The Transitioning Stage of the Conversation Framework before presenting your opportunity.

DISCOVERING STAGE CONVERSATION GUIDELINE!

On the following page is an outline of some of the questions that have been covered in this chapter. This is a basic structure that you can use in any situation, though in this case I have associated it with work and the workplace. Though it's impossible to cover every available question in this book, use the ones on the Guideline as a base, and expand on the answers you get to them. Also, comb through the book and compile your own expanded version of the Guideline.

You don't have to use all the questions. Use the ones that are relevant and, if some seem uncomfortable for you, such as the feeling ones, give yourself a push and say them anyway. The results both for you and the other person will be priceless.

Natural Selling®
Discovering Stage Conversation Guideline!

<u>Background Questions</u>
(What is your Present Situation?)
"What kind of work do you do?"
"How long have you been doing it?"
"What drew you into this type of work?"

<u>Needs Awareness/Development Questions</u>
(Is your Present Situation working for you?) Likes and dislikes.
"Do you like what you're doing?"
"What do you like/don't you like about your work?"
"Why do you like/don't like . . . (What you just told me)?"

"Is there anything else you like/don't like about your work?"
"Why do you like/don't like . . . (What you just told me)?"
"Why is doing/not doing all of that important to you?"
"How do you feel about doing/not doing that?"

"What would you change about your job if you could?"

"Why would you change . . . ?"

"Why is that important to you? (What would that do for you?)"

"How do you feel about that?"

"Is there anything else you do/don't care about, and would change?"

"How does that make you feel to have/not to have what you just said you wanted?"

"What would you rather be doing if you could?"

"How would that make you feel if you could do that?"

"What's stopping you from getting what you want?"

Consequence Questions

(What if you make an incorrect decision?)

"What if . . . ?"

"What will you do if you cannot . . .?"

Solution Questions

(What would you do to change your present situation?)

"What have you done about it, if anything?"

"Have you looked for anything that would give you what you're seeking?"

"What would you do about it if you could?"

"Why is that?"

"Why is that important to you?" (How do you see the benefits of solving your problem?)

"What's preventing you from making a change or doing it right now?"

<u>Qualifying Questions</u>

(Are you prepared to change your present situation?)

"Let me ask you, if something came along that would give you all the things you wanted, such as (repeat the logical and emotional dreams and desires) and none of the things you don't like, such as (repeat the negatives) would you look at an opportunity like that?"

AN EXAMPLE OF A DIALOGUE

The following is an example of what a conversation looks like. This conversation is in the context of talking with a stranger. However, the process and many of the questions would be the same no matter who the other person is.

Some of the questions in the Natural Selling® Conversation Guideline have not been included as they are not relevant to the conversation. It underlies that you only use the ones you need. The circumstances of the conversation are those of talking with a stranger. The replies to the questions have enough information to take the conversation a lot further, and if this was a real conversation I would. But space, and the complexity of putting it on paper, does not allow me the luxury to do that. So take it as a given that I might not conclude so hastily with all the great information given me. All the answers have further information behind them and finding out more would broaden and then deepen the base and, subsequently, the relationship.

I've kept the conversation going in a linear fashion, though conversations rarely work out this way – would it be that people were so obliging. I've also kept as closely as I can to the same questions in the Guideline so you can identify them easily. However, in real life the questions would probably be phrased differently to reflect the context and uniqueness of the conversation. There are many ways to ask the same question, as you will discover with experience. Just learn the basic ones and the right words will come.

BACKGROUND QUESTIONS

"Are you presently working?"

– "Yes, I am!"

"What kind of work do you do?"

– "I work full time as a chef."

"How long have you been doing it?"

– "About 22 years."

"Was this your first job?"

– "Yes, I started straight from college."

"What drew you into this type of work?"

– "I enjoyed cooking and figured I could travel the world as a chef if I mastered it."

NEEDS AWARENESS/DEVELOPMENT QUESTIONS

"Do you still enjoy doing it after 22 years?"

– "I love it on one hand, but, well, you know how it is!"

"What part of the job do you like the most?"

– "Well, I like the fact that I work in a good restaurant and have people appreciate my food."

"I sense that's important to you?"

– "Yes, It's nice to be recognized for the effort I put in."

"Anything else you like about it?"

– "Yes, the freedom to create what dishes I like!"

"Sounds interesting. What in particular do you like about that?"

– "Well, it gives me a feeling of independence and creativity."

"Is that important to you?"

– "Yes, it is! I think having self-worth is always important, don't you?"

"Yes, I do! How do you find it makes you feel when you have that? "

– "A sense of achievement – pride, I guess!"

"Would you change anything about your job as a chef if you could?"

– "I sure would – the irregular hours, and the money. The money is very good, but there is never enough to pay off past debts I have."

"How do you feel about that?"

– "Trapped! I can't afford to leave, because the working conditions wouldn't change much elsewhere, so it's a little frustrating and not so fulfilling anymore."

"Is there anything else you would change?"

– "No! That's pretty much it, I think."

"Is being a chef still your passion or would you rather be doing something else if you could?"

– "Actually, the truth is I would rather get out of the business. My heart is in working with a kids' project I've been heavily involved in for the past few years. It's a special needs group for children in Hawaii and I'd love to be able to raise funds and build a healing center for them."

"How would that make you feel if you could do that?"

– "Wonderful! It's a real passion of mine. There's nothing better than helping and watching those kids pick themselves up and making something of themselves."

"So, what's stopping you from getting what you "want?"

– "I can't afford it and I've no idea how to get beyond that."

CONSEQUENCE QUESTIONS

"What will you do if you can't realize this dream of yours?"

– "I don't know! I worry about it a lot. I'm moving on in years and I can't imagine being a chef for the rest of my life."

SOLUTION QUESTIONS

"Have you looked for any work that would give you what you're seeking – the extra money and more time?"

– "Yes, but I haven't found anything that is flexible enough to fit my irregular hours."

"What would you do if you could?"

– "I've no idea at this point – like I said, everything I looked at doesn't give me the flexible – it's a little frustrating!"

"What's preventing you from making a change or doing it right now, apart from not finding the right thing?"

– "Nothing except there seems to be nothing around and I don't think I have the skills to do anything else."

QUALIFYING QUESTION

"Well, let me ask you something. If something came along that fitted in with the hours you are working and allowed you to get the extra money you wanted, so you could pay off your debts and feel you were moving toward achieving your dream of building the care center – would you look at an opportunity like that?"

– "All the time! Why? Do you know of something?"

Your conversation can take many different routes. You probably noticed there are other issues and clues in the conversation that could be developed. It's up to you to develop the strongest ones that will serve both of you. The beauty in this approach is that each conversation is unique and yet the process is the same.

At the end of The Discovering Stage, after having fully explored your potential partner's logical and emotional needs, you will know if they have recognized the need for change and if they possess the desire to make a change: If they do, now is the moment to reveal to them how you can help by presenting your opportunity.

CHAPTER 13

Stage 3: The Transitioning Stage

*Men honor what lies within the sphere of their
knowledge but they do not realize how dependent
they are on what lies beyond it.* – Chuang-Tse

When you have a clear picture of what your potential partner wants and whether they are prepared to make a change to get it, you now make the transition from focusing on asking questions and listening to demonstrating how you can help. The Transitioning Stage quietly, gently, and without fanfare, opens the door to The Presenting Stage. It's like inviting someone to come through the gate of your garden because you discover you both like plants and flowers and you have a wealth of them to show.

It's a very simple process. You just simply offer the idea that you have the solution:

"Well, based on what you told me, I'm doing something that might be what you're looking for. If you're interested I would be happy to share that with you!"

It's important to begin the sentence with the phrase, *'Based on what you told me,'* whenever you can because it makes the point that you're going to say something you didn't make up – the other person said it. It prepares the groundwork for what you're going to present being based on everything you were told.

The question is without a question mark. It's a soft statement of invitation. You will get mostly 'Yes' answers for there is no reason for the other person not to say, 'Yes!' After all, all you're doing is offering them a solution to get what they want.

The degree of 'Yes' will vary, from being somewhat guarded to outright enthusiasm. Take into account that while many people are motivated to do something to make a change, they might not want to make a wholesale change. They could only be interested in doing something part time. Part time or full time, at the end of the day you're looking for a committed partner, no matter what level they decide to participate in.

Having opened the doors to get approval, you then 'pull it all together' in the next stage by presenting the correct solution.

Natural Selling®

Part V

Principle #4:
Feeding Back What You Think You Heard They Want

Chapter 14:
The Presenting Stage

Chapter 15:
The Committing Stage

HOW TO SELL NETWORK MARKETING

231

CHAPTER 14

Stage 4: The Presenting Stage

Do not conquer the world with force, for force
only causes resistance. – Tao Te Ching

You've already discovered in chapter 9, the mechanics behind *what* to present. As you know, it's a matter of understanding how to relate the problem someone has to the *relevant* features, advantages and benefits of your business opportunity that will solve it for them. In this chapter you will expand on this and learn further *how* to present your business opportunity.

SUMMARY AND AGREEMENT

The Summary and Agreement is the ultimate in feedback and summarizing. This is where you shine by acting as a sounding board for the other person!

You summarize what you have heard by tying together all the factual and feeling needs, to confirm you have a complete understanding of their problem. You then present your solution and ask if that is what they are looking for.

PRESENTING YOUR SOLUTION TO SATISFY THE NEEDS

This is a combination of presenting and asking for a commitment to move forward. It's all done quietly with inner enthusiasm and confidence. This energy will show through as you demonstrate your competency. Here is how it works:

- Summarize the main logical and personal problems.
- Explain briefly what you do.
- Present your solution with the *specific* features – their advantages and benefits that will solve their problems.
- Ask a qualifying question.

I've expanded on the above process to give you key phrases you can use for your presentation. You don't have to use these words necessarily, just understand their intent. Use your own if you wish. Vary the approach depending on the person you're talking with and the circumstances, such as if you're calling a lead.

The main thing to remember here is you can present the above in any way you like. Do whatever is most comfortable and easy for you. Just learn the format so that when you need it, the words will flow in the manner they are meant to. It doesn't have to be precise. The fact that you are doing it puts you far ahead of anything that anyone else has done.

SUMMARIZE THE MAIN PROBLEMS

"You know how you said . . . ." (Repeat what is missing or what they would really like to do.)

"And . . . ." (Repeat an important logical problem.)

"And because of this it's making you feel . . . ." (Repeat an important emotional problem.)

EXPLAIN BRIEFLY WHAT YOU DO

"Well, what I do is . . . ."

PRESENT YOUR BUSINESS OPPORTUNITY

"What this means to you is you can do the same thing! You can . . . ." (Describe the advantages of the specific features of your business opportunity that will satisfy the logical side of their problem.)

"Which will allow you to . . . ." (Describe the benefits of the same features that will satisfy the personal side of their problem.)

ASK A QUALIFYING QUESTION

"Does that sound/feel/look as if it might take care of what you want?"

That's it! When you ask the last question, be quiet and wait for the response. Whatever response you receive, such as, "Looks interesting, what is it, tell me more about it?" or "Yes, I'd love to!" – you then move on and talk about the company, the products, and how you got involved.

So here is what a full presentation might look like drawn from the conversation in chapter 12 with the chef.

*"**You know how you said** you would like to pursue your dream of creating a healing center for children in Hawaii **and** you can't, because you're working irregular hours as a chef and you don't have any time or money to pay off your debts, to make your ambition come true."*

*"**And because of this, it's making you feel** trapped and unfulfilled?"*

*"**Well, what I do is,** I work for myself in my own home-based business. I work my own hours – can come and go as I please, make a very good income, whether I work or not – and can work mostly anywhere I like!"*

*"**What this means to you is** that you could do the same thing. You could do what I'm doing on a part-time basis, when it is convenient to you, so you would have the security of your present job until you are exceeding your present income and can leave it to pursue your dream of building the healing center you were talking about. Not only that, the ongoing income you get, whether you're working or not, will pay for all your living costs while you set up and operate your center!"*

*"**This will allow you** to get the fulfillment back you said you were looking for, and let you start feeling good about yourself again, by getting your dream moving forward."*

*"Does that **sound/feel/look** as if it might take care of what you want?"*

In this scenario, you can see how all the main factual and personal problems are resolved by the business opportunity which is explained by way of its features and their advantages and benefits.

When the other person says, 'Yes!' You can explain more about the company and products, and move toward a commitment to action.

If you don't get it quite right, that's okay. People will help you. They'll be delighted that you understand so much. And, besides, you will have done what only 2% of successful professional salespeople do and, that is, demonstrate you have been listening!

You will notice there was no mention of products or use of technical or industry language. *People are not so interested in what it is, but what it can do for them.* They will buy from you because you have understood and listened to them.

THE SANDWICH TEST!

I remember going through this process with a potential partner when I was in Jacksonville Beach, training some distributors there. I was having lunch with him having rented a car from his company two days previously. Prior to lunch I had three contacts with him. The first was the day I rented the car, when he asked me some personal questions for the rental agreement. Because he asked me questions, I felt 'obliged' to ask him some too! (Except my questions were different from his.) The second contact was when I called him the next day. I reflected on something interesting he had said about what he really wanted out of life, and would he like to have lunch to talk about it, and discuss how we might achieve that. He agreed saying that he had one hour and we set the place to meet at a local deli two days later. The third contact was when I phoned to confirm lunch

During lunch I asked the types of questions you learned in this book, and presented the idea of how he could get what he wanted, using the same format as above. His response was, "I'm not sure what this is all about, but it sounds cool! What's the next step?" You will get reactions like this. It makes the point that it's not so much telling people what it is, but how your business opportunity will help people get what they really want.

The sandwich? Well, I noticed 40 minutes into the conversation that I had finished my sandwich some 10 minutes earlier (an 8" Vegetarian Sub) and all he had taken was two bites of his. The moral of the story is: When you're asking questions and listening you have plenty of time to eat!

CHAPTER 15

Stage 5: The Committing Stage

Address the other person as a person, and you will
solve their logical as well as their personal needs.

The commitment to move forward is a natural, casual step from The Presenting Stage. It takes two forms:

1. A commitment to take a series of intermediate action steps.

2. A commitment to become a partner.

Anything less is a signal that they are unlikely to go with you or your proposed solution. If that is the case, this might be the time to ask more questions or to move on to other opportunities.

These are the types of steps you are likely to go through when discussing your business opportunity.

STEP 1. AN OVERVIEW

Give a brief overview of you, your company and your products. Relate as many of the features of your business opportunity as you can to your previous discussions, though you don't have to go into a lot of detail. As new information or perhaps concerns come to light, talk about them using your Natural Selling® skills by going over the Discovering Stage again in the Conversational Framework.

STEP 2. MAKE A SUGGESTION!

You'll come to a point where you need to decide on one of two action steps. Either ask for the commitment to join you, or make a suggestion to set up a process of further discovery for them to move progressively toward making a final decision.

If you decide to ask for the full commitment, you can progress to 'The Final Step' in this chapter. If your prospective partner needs to find out more, then you can offer one of a number of next step options. It's different for everyone. Only you will know based on your previous dialogue. *Whatever you do – ask for the commitment to do something!* If the other person needs to take progressive steps toward assessing your offer, this is where you *selectively* use the sales tools that are available to you. Only use what is relevant and what they need. Start this journey by making a statement and asking a question:

"I'd like to suggest as the next step that . . . ."

- We review information on the website
- We look more closely at the products
- We look more closely at the business opportunity
- We meet some other people in my organization
- We get a video or audio tape or brochure into your hands
- You take a training workshop
- We attend an opportunity meeting together

"What would be most appropriate for you?"

You could also throw it open and ask them what next step they would like to take. Involve the other person as much as possible.

Always ensure you both make commitments to do something by a certain time. And always follow up; otherwise you will be letting the other person down.

Continually Check For Agreement

Don't take anything for granted as you progress with your discussion. Check all the time for mutual agreement to ensure understanding. Some people don't like to admit they don't know things, so gently help them. Ask questions like:

"Is that clear or would you like me to run over that again?"

"Do you like this part of the program?"

"Do you see the value in all of this for you?"

"Will this be worthwhile?"

CHECK FOR ANY CONCERNS

The same importance must be given to potential concerns. It's likely that some 'concerns' will arise. A concern can be something real. Discuss it. If you hide from it, it will still be there. It might also haunt you later on. You have a good relationship, so ask if there are any concerns and bring them onto the table. If there are, talk about them as two people working together to resolve them. Continually check by asking questions like:

"How does this look so far?"

"Are you comfortable with this?"

"Do you have anything you would like to address at this point?"

Don't assume people will voice concerns. *Prepare* for the most common of them, but *don't expect* them, otherwise the energy in your words will reflect this. Keep your conversations positive and leave out the negative thoughts. People are not thinking what you think they think – only you are!

CONCERNS ARE NOT OBJECTIONS

A concern is not an objection or rejection of you! Don't handle it as if it were, otherwise you are likely to lose what you both have gained. Now is not the time to sell or persuade. It's the time to discuss using the same principles and methods when you learned to have a dialogue. If you have done your work correctly, all the objections will be eliminated during The Discovering Stage.

HELPING THEM RESOLVE THEIR CONCERNS

When someone expresses a concern, make sure you Clarify, Discuss and help them Challenge it, if it's appropriate. Use this conversational framework to help you.

CLARIFY

Make sure you understand the concern or the question. Don't assume you know what's behind it, or tell them you 'know how they feel because you used to feel that way and you found it to be something different.' That is objection handling where you are answering with a, "Yes, BUT!" answer. I guarantee you don't know how they feel, unless they have told you previously. Find out by asking!

"When you say . . . (Repeat what they said,) what do you mean by that?"

Here are some other questions you can tag on to the end of, "When you say . . ."

"Why do you ask that?"

"Can I ask where you got that information from?"

"How did you arrive at that?"

DISCUSS

This is where you will talk about whatever the issue is using The Discovering Stage of Conversation Framework again to uncover and explore. Solution Questions are especially powerful here. Ask them how they see resolving the concern. People can become very creative when they're self-interested.

CHALLENGE

After you've discussed the concern and you know that it is one based on a belief that might not be serving them, or based on an experience that you know, while true, could be otherwise, make a suggestion:

"Suppose it wasn't what you thought it was?"

"What if we could . . . ?"

"What if you could . . . ?"

"Suppose you could . . . ?"

. . . and offer an alternative view to theirs, such as, *"What if you could get the training you said you needed that would help you succeed?"* Most people will be interested in continuing to listen. They might not have any choice but to go with your solution so they will be looking for your help to overcome their concerns and replace the history that created the concern.

One of the more common concerns is a fear of selling. Here is how you can respond to it. You can use the same process with other concerns if they arise. Respond to the concern of, "I could never sell!" and ask your questions conversationally, not as a script:

"I can appreciate that! Let me ask you? When you say 'You could never sell,' what do you mean by that?"

– "Well, the whole idea of selling to people things they don't want is something I could never do!"

"I'm curious. What is your perception of selling, or what do you think selling is all about?"

– "You know, all that persuading . . . I could never do that!"

"I can understand that! I have to agree with you there. Can I ask, do you feel I've sold you or was persuasive with you while we've been talking?"

– "Actually, no, I don't . . . ."

"And yet, during the time we've spent together, you've told me all about yourself and what you're looking for and we came up something that could possibly help you get what you want. Is that right?"

– "Yes!"

"Well, <u>suppose selling wasn't what you thought it was</u>? Suppose it was doing what we are doing: talking with people and discovering if you can be of help? What if you could learn how to do that, and even let what you learn spill over

into your personal life as well, to strengthen the relation-
ships you have and help you create new ones, would you
consider learning how to do that with me?"

– "I never thought about it that way. Yes, I would be open
to knowing what it takes."

You can see how by never making a statement, and using
what you know to ask questions, how people can persuade
themselves to look at things differently. You can use this process with any concern that comes up!

STEP 3. KEEP MAKING SUGGESTIONS!

Repeat one or more of the previous steps on the list in Step
2 that are relevant to moving the process forward to help your
potential partner come to an informed decision. Ask:

"What would you like to have a look at next? Would you like
to . . .?" – until you cover everything of interest.

Get them involved in the process. Different people move at
different speeds. Pace yourself and them. It can take many
mini steps before the final one!

THE FORTUNE IS IN THE FOLLOW UP!

Follow up! Follow up! Follow up! Always make sure you
have set a time and date to follow up on. Use the S.M.A.R.T.
formula to help you: Specific: Measurable: Attainable: Reason-
able: Timely. Set specific objectives and leave your discussion
with statements such as:

"So I'll call you at 7 P.M. next Tuesday and when we get to-
gether you'll have listened to the tape I'll send you and we'll be
able to discuss specific aspects of it."

And make sure you call. There is no reason for you not to!
They are expecting it and you need to stay congruent with the
integrity of your previous conversations.

Step 4. The Final Step

Make a suggestion and ask a final question:

"Well, we seem to have covered the basis of what you're looking for. I'm not sure there is anything more I can show you, so . . . ."

"How about getting you registered while we're together so you can start moving toward having the things you want?"

You can use these questions as well to add flavor to your endings!

"Why don't we put together a plan for you to get you up and running?"

"When would you like to be up and running?"

"Why don't we just get you started?"

"When would be a good time to get together and start moving this forward for you?"

And there you have it. One more motivated, happy partner!

Part VI

Chapter 16:
Endings And Beginnings

Gratitudes

CHAPTER 16

Endings And Beginnings

Find your own truth, by shedding the truths of others
that prevent you from having the freedom and abundance
that is your universal right.

Perhaps in this book you have found *your* 'truth' by matching, strengthening or altering your beliefs. It's all about who you are, not what you're selling. You could have the best business opportunity in the world, but what good is it if your potential partners need to get over *you* to get to *it*?

Now it's up to you to take action and use what you need to make it work for you and for the people who will become your successful associates and customers.

Ultimately the success of your endeavors will be determined by the strength of your belief in what you are doing, and the strength of your action. The only way I know to get to the next horizon is a willingness to continually take action based on a willingness to continually learn and a desire to succeed. These are the hallmarks of success.

I invite you to take all-out massive positive action and reap the inner and material rewards that are sitting there waiting for you. The journey is continually ending and beginning. Let a Zen saying help you on that journey: *'Wherever you are, you are the master.'*

GRATITUDES

Since I started training and coaching distributors, associates and wellness consultants, a large number of people entered into my life, and helped Natural Selling® and myself grow. Their encouragement, support, hospitality and friendship have enlightened and taught me more than any books I've read. The following people have certainly been great companions on the road to fulfillment. Many still travel the road with me, and for that I'm grateful!

Maggie McKee, Dr. Myron Wentz, Rick Tonita, Clarence Joy, Jeff Meyers, Peg Ostby, Kevin Kiernen, Mark Crowley, Guan Lim, Paula Harker and Kyle Tourand, Shane Klipness, Joe Lancelot, Alan Hollender, Melissa Neuwirth, Dr. Ray and Elizabeth Strand, Geoff Gosson, Russell and Rita Haack, Carol Gordon, Yvonne Copeland, Sandy and Keith Moreland, Christian Bash, Marg & Martyn Clarke, Les Raketti, Dr. David Silverman, Wendy Lucas, Karla Kos, John Kehoe, Tom Baker, Heather Trondsen, Dr. Chuck Misja, Jim Britt, Michael Losier, Jeannie and Gordon Williams, Carolyn Keith, Susan Ormrod, Ken Kelonko, Judy and Ned Powell, Mike Lewis, Kathy O'Brien, Rick Grossberg, Daryl Austman, Pete and Sarah Wiggins, Nancy Thompson, Gerry Aikin, Brock Tully, Samantha Brinkley, Michael D'Avolio, John and Chris Mortimer, Paul Sterling, Sandra Sternberg, James Downie, Doris Wood, Steve McGuire, Karl Jacobsen, Mike Vandermark, Peter Brook, Geoffrey Lane, Penny Manser, Harv Eker, Rick Provost, Bill Mackie, and, from my heart, my gratitude to my wife Sandy, for being the wise spirit that she is!

Michael Oliver, January 2002

For Your <u>FREE</u> Website Support and Resources…

Log On NOW!

www.NaturalSelling.com

Want to keep your new skills refreshed and fine-tuned… want to continue removing old habits…?

- Register for Michael's FREE 'Naturally Speaking' sales tips newsletter delivered directly to your computer.
- Listen online to a FREE 1-hour Introduction to Natural Selling®.
- Register for a Free 'LIVE' Interactive Introduction to Natural Selling® TeleClass.
- Learn about upcoming Workshops, TeleClasses, Books and Audios.

PLUS… Download the following …

- Natural Selling® sales tools and charts to assist you in your business and personal life.
- Online audios to experience new concepts in Dialogue
- Interviews with Michael
- Past articles
- Online transcripts
- And much more….

Like to Have Michael Train YOU in Person?

www.NaturalSelling.com
Info@NaturalSelling.com

WORKSHOPS

"Experiential... Intense... Interactive!" This is how Michael's workshops have been described. Details and schedule on website. Privately sponsored workshops are available upon request.

SPEAKING

Michael's ability to speak about how to *effectively* and *practically* apply 'out of the box' thinking is legendary. Your team and associates will be *informed* and *inspired* to achieve greater results both in their personal and professional lives. To request Michael to speak at your event, meeting or convention, please email or call.

TELECLASSES TRAINING

Michael offers a variety of TeleConferencing Training and Coaching classes for the beginner to the advanced.

AUDIOS CURRENTLY AVAILABLE

The Best of Michael Oliver's 6-Day Fast Track TeleClasses.
12 Ways To Start Effective Conversations Without Fear

1.800.758.6989
1.775.886.0777

502 N. Division St.
Carson City, NV
89703 USA

HOW TO SELL NETWORK MARKETING

ABOUT THE AUTHOR

Michael Oliver is the founder of **Natural Selling® Sales Training**. He is an international sales trainer, speaker, writer and coach with over 25 years of experience in direct sales and sales training, focused on helping people achieve exceptional results.

His teleconference training, coaching, on-site workshops and speeches are in demand around the world.

Michael's practical skills in sales development, facilitation and training, have helped Companies and tens of thousands of Distributors and Direct Salespeople worldwide.

He practically demonstrates how you can dramatically improve your individual results by understanding how to help others improve theirs. By applying the philosophies of ancient wisdoms of communicating from the soul with the pragmatic requirements of the modern world, Michael empowers Distributors by giving them the people skills needed to attract new associates and customers.

Michael concludes,

"People will no longer accept being persuaded to buy. Your business has to manifest that you're in it for them . . . not you! And you have to live and breathe that belief."

To learn more about Michael, visit his website at...

www.NaturalSelling.com